Anatomy and Pl Laboratory Manual

Instructor: Dr. Krista Howarth

Instructional Assistant: Adrienne Tearle
tearlea@mcmaster.ca
x 23565

Lab Technician: Christiane DeSavigny
desavig@mcmaster.ca
x 21842 or x 26867 in the lab

Welcome to the laboratory portion of Anatomy and Physiology.

Before participating in any laboratories, you are responsible for ensuring that you have attended an anatomy lab orientation. This orientation will be offered during your first scheduled lab. You MUST sign an agreement in order to enter the anatomy lab. You will also have to sign a document stating you have participated in a Site Specific WHMIS.

Anatomy Act and Orientation

The Anatomy Act of Ontario is administered by the Chief Coroner of Ontario. This piece of legislation regulates access to the Anatomy Lab and requires that appropriate care and procedures be used when working with human material. In order to meet this requirement, the Education Programme in Anatomy requires an orientation for those who will be using the area and its resources. Students should be aware of:
1. The Anatomy Act and the regulations governing Access to the Anatomy Lab, which is a restricted area, and;
2. The procedures required for the proper use and care of the specimens and other resources.

Students must attend an orientation to Anatomy before using the Anatomy area. Abuse of resources or access will result in withdrawal of privileges.

Every person who contravenes this Act is guilty of an offence and on conviction is liable, if a corporation, to a fine of not more than $2,000 or, if not a corporation, to a fine of not more than $1,000 or to imprisonment for a term of not more than one year, or to both. R.S.O. 1990, c. A.21, s. 13 (1).

Rules for the Anatomy Lab

1.   Access to the Anatomy Lab

Access to the IAHS 451 lab is restricted. The IAHS 451 lab is under video surveillance. The door will be open when you arrive and will lock when lab begins. You must be punctual and present at the lab introduction in order to participate in the lab.

2.   Handling specimens.

Handling the blocks. These specimens are the most durable components of the permanent collection; however they will scratch and shatter if dropped or mishandled.

Handling specimens floating in preserving fluid: these specimens are delicate. The containers that they are in often leak and are fragile. Do not shake these specimens.

Handling plastinated specimens: these specimens are subject to damage when they are pulled upon or forced to move beyond the limitations of the preserved tendons and ligaments. Please do not force the joints or pull on the various features demonstrated in these specimens.

Handling wet specimens: Wear gloves when handling these specimens. Remove them from their wrapping or container and put them on a tray. Do not pull on any aspect of the specimen or force a joint to move through its range of motion. Do not attempt to investigate structures lying deep to the exposed structures. There are other wet specimens that demonstrate the deeper structures. When finished, put the specimen back, cover it with the cloth and soak the cloth with moisturizing fluid. Clean the tray and cart or counter with cart cleaner.

-Do not move specimens around the lab.

-No food or drink in the lab space.

-Closed toes shoes and a lab coat must be worn at all times in the lab.

-Do not remove ANYTHING from the lab space.

-NO cameras or other recording devices are permitted in the lab.

-Cell phones must be turned OFF and kept in your school bag (i.e. not with you at the lab station)

-Clean up after yourself. Put your gloves in the garbage and put all specimens, models and trays away.

-As a courtesy, please move your lab stools back under the table when your lab is finished.

-f you have an accident or need assistance please contact a member of the staff or call emergency at 88.

1. Klee Wyck → laughing one

2. Sophie's babies → cemetery mounds

3. totem poles → tribal culture

→ 4. ~~teaching~~ missionaries→ necessary skills to white
ckt

— 5. roman ⇄ Kleewyick or collection of short stores?

6. totem poles → outlaw to eradicate native culture

7. Nativ̲e̲ training schools → outlawed use of native language

8. Klee wyck → effects of colonization

9. Studies field → heroism attitude

10. Break of Day in the trenches → Isaac Rosenberg

11. German's Dream Bed → inquiry into causes of war

12. Ach, ist Schwtsch denk'ne → horror of war

13. Galachys → unable to understand narrator's guilt

→ 14. "the sacrifice" → a̲b̲s̲u̲r̲d̲i̲t̲y̲ of human or god's involvement in history

15 lorry ride → cause of war

16. General demoralizes enemy.

Site Specific Laboratory Safety Guidleines

1. Notify your instructor immediately if you are pregnant, colour blind, allergic to insects or chemicals, taking immunosuppressant drugs, or have other medical conditions (such as diabetes or immunological defect) that may require you to take special precautions in the lab.
2. Upon entering the laboratory, place all books, coats, purses, backpacks, etc. in designated areas, not on the bench tops.
3. Locate, and when appropriate, learn to use exits, fire extinguisher, fire blanket, chemical shower, eyewash, first aid kit, broken glass container, and cleanup materials for spills.
4. In case of fire, evacuate the room and assemble outside the building.
5. Do not eat, drink, smoke or apply cosmetics or touch your eyes, nose or mouth while in the lab.
6. Confine all long hair, loose clothing, and dangling jewelry.
7. Wear closed toed shoes at all times while in the laboratory.
8. Cover any cuts or scrapes with a sterile, water-proof bandage while in the lab.
9. Wear eye protection when working with chemicals.
10. Never pipette by mouth. Use mechanical pipetting devises.
11. Wash skin immediately and thoroughly if contaminated.
12. Do not perform unauthorized experiments.
13. Do not use equipment without instruction.
14. Report ALL spills and accidents to the instructor.
15. Never leave heat sources unattended.
16. Keep chemicals away from direct heat or sunlight.
17. Do not allow any liquid to come into contact with electrical cords. Handle electrical cords with dry hands. Do not attempt to disconnect electrical equipment that crackles, snaps or smokes.
18. Upon completion of the laboratory exercise, place all materials in the disposal areas designated by your instructor. Dispose of gloves in the garbage unless instructed otherwise.
19. When handling potentially biohazardous materials, gloves are to be placed in the designated biohazard receptacles.
20. Do not pick up broken glassware with your hands. Use the broom and dust pan and dispose of it in the broken glass container. Never put broken glass in a garbage can.
21. Wear disposable gloves when working with blood, other body fluids or mucous membranes. Change gloves after possible contamination and wash hands immediately after gloves are removed.
22. Leave the laboratory clean and organized for the next student. Please move your lab stools back under the benches before leaving the lab.
23. Wash your hands before leaving the laboratory.

Safety Alert
McMaster University

Universal Precautions Applying to Blood, Bodily Fluids, and Tissues

1. Gloves, lab coats, and protective eyewear must be worn when coming in contact with blood or bodily fluids.

2. Wash hands when contaminated or immediately after gloves are removed.
3. Take precautions to avoid injuries with sharp instruments.

4. NEVER RECAP NEEDLES.

5. Use only mechanical pipetting devices.

6. Use biological safety cabinet or fume hood whenever procedures involve bending, sonicating, or vigorously shaking with may generate aerosols.

7. Decontaminate work surfaces daily after spills. Use 1 to 10 household bleach, 70% ethanol, or alternative germicide. Dispose of glass or paper in yellow plastic bags and dispose of plastics in pink plastic bags.

8. Remove all lab coats or other protective equipment before leaving the lab.

9. Decontaminate all equipment prior to repair or relocation.

10. Hepatitis B vaccine or other relevant vaccinations are recommended.

17. Animal farm → satire
18. Animal farm → Russian revolution

19. Language → political control
20. maintaining (orwell) power depends on mass ignorance
21. "Pravda" truth

22. Raven → religion

23. propaganda → Squeaker
24. "Internationale" → Socialist song

25 "beasts of england" is parody of "internationale"
26. "theater of the absurd" → absence of universal meaning
27. Endgame is written after WW2

28. Clar sees desolation outside

Kinesiology 1AA3/1YY3/2YY3

29. Hannm Res to his Inter This "accused"

30. Ih enforce, life is a game to which there is no meaningful end

31. Apartheid → defined legal relationship between South Africa and white people

32. Apartheid laws → protect

● Safety Notes for the PowerLab

Product Intention

PowerLab systems have been designed only for use in teaching and research applications. They are not intended for clinical or critical lifecare use should never be used for these purposes, nor for the prevention, diagnosis, curing, treatment, or alleviation of disease, injury, or handicap.

Applicable Safety Standards

When used with insulated transducers or ADInstruments isolated front-ends, PowerLab systems are safe for human connection. The ML132 Bio Amp, ML135 Dual Bio Amp, ML408 Dual Bio Amp/Stimulator, ML116 GSR Amp, ML117 BP Amp and ML180 front ends conform to international safety requirements. Specifically, these requirements are IEC601-1 and its addenda (Table S–1), and various harmonised standards worldwide (UL2601.1 in the USA, and AS/NZS3200.1 in Australia and New Zealand). In accordance with European standards they also comply with the electromagnetic compatibility requirements under EN60601-1, which encompasses the EMC directive. Further information is available on request.

EC Standard No.	EC Standard No. International Standard — Medical electrical equipment
IEC601-1:1988	General requirements for safety
IEC601-1-1:1992	Safety requirements for medical electrical systems
IEC601-1-2:1993	Electromagnetic compatibility

Table S–1
Applicable safety standards met by ADInstruments isolated front-ends

General Safety Instructions

• Since the PowerLab is used in conjunction with a computer (which has much higher leakage currents) the subject must be at least 1.83 metres (6 feet) away from any of the equipment, to avoid contact with the computer. The Bio Amp or BP Amp cable provides enough distance. Alternatively, an isolation transformer can be used to supply power to both the PowerLab and the computer.

• The PowerLab 2/20 and PowerLab 4/20 are classified as Class I medical equipment, which means that protection against electricshock in the event of a fault relies on a direct connection through the power cable to your building's earth conductor. The power cable supplied with your PowerLab provides the required ground connection to the power outlet. If your building does not have power outlet sockets with a good ground connection, then you may use the ground connection on the rear of the PowerLab to provide the equipotential connection to the building's earth conductor. A ground connection is an essential part of this equipment's safety. Never use the PowerLab without a ground connection.

Safety Symbol Explanation

Every ADInstruments device designed for connection to humans, including the Bio Amp, BP Amp, GSR Amp and Stimulus Isolator, carries one or more of three safety symbols, as shown in Figure S–1. These symbols appear next to those input and output connectors that can be directly connected to human subjects.

The three symbols are:

•

BF (body protected) symbol

. This means that the input connectors are suitable for connection to humans provided there is no direct electrical connection to the heart.

•

Warning symbol

. The exclamation mark inside a triangle means that you should consult the supplied documentation (you're reading it) for operating information or cautionary and safety information before using the device.

•

CF (cardiac protected) symbol

(Appears on some models of Bio Amp, and every BP Amp.) This means that the input connectors are suitable for connection to humans even when there is direct electrical connection to the heart.

Cleaning and Sterilization

This system is not supplied with materials or components likely to need sterilization. If you need to clean peripherals likely to be in contact with different subjects, they can be cold-sterilized with an appropriate sterilizing agent. No part of the system can be autoclaved.

Storage

It is recommended that the hardware be kept below 40°C and above 0°C in a moisture-free or low-humidity environment when not in use (storage only). Electronic components are susceptible to corrosive substances and atmospheres, so it is also advisable to keep the system away from laboratory chemicals.

Preventative Inspection and Maintenance

Both PowerLab systems and ADInstruments front-ends are maintenance free and do not require periodic calibration or adjustment to ensure medical safety. Internal diagnostic software performs system checks during power up and will report errors if a significant problem is found. There is no need to open the instrument for inspection or maintenance, and doing so within the warranty period will void the warranty.

If you so wish, your PowerLab system can be periodically checked for basic medical safety by using an appropriate medical safety testing device. Tests such as earth leakage, earth bond, insulation resistance, patient leakage and auxiliary currents and power cable integrity can all be performed on the PowerLab system without having to remove the covers. You should follow the instructions for the testing device if performing such tests. If the PowerLab system is found not to comply with such testing you should contact your PowerLab dealer to arrange for the equipment to be checked and serviced. You should not attempt to service the device yourself.

Bio Amp Safety Instructions

The Bio Amp inputs of the ML760 Powerlab / 4ST and ML860 Powerlab 4 / 20T and the ML132 Bio Amp, ML 135 Dual Bio Amp and ML 408 Dual Bio Amp Stimulator, are electrically isolated from the mains supply in order to prevent current flow that could result in injury to the subject. Several points must be observed for safe operation of the Bio Amp.

1. Each Bio Amp is supplied with a 3-lead or a 5-lead Bio Amp subject cable and lead wire system that meets the safety requirements of the IEC601-1 medical standard. This cable is fully insulated and is manufactured with special leads and plugs to prevent accidental connection to power supply sockets. Bio Amps are safe for human connection if used with the supplied subject cables and lead wires.
2. The Bio Amp inputs of the PowerLab are not defibrillator protected. Using the Bio Amp to record signals during defibrillator discharges may damage the input stages of the amplifiers. This may result in a safety hazard.
3. Subjects, Bio Amp cables and lead wires should be kept well away from power supply cabling. This also helps reduce power supply interference with recorded signals.
4. Never use damaged Bio Amp cables or leads. Damaged cables and leads must always be replaced before any connection to humans is made.

Isolated Stimulator Instructions

The Isolated Stimulator outputs of the ML760 PowerLab / 4ST and ML860 PowerLab 4/ 20 T, and the outputs of the ML180 Stimulus Isolator and ML408 Dual Bio Amp / Stimulator, although electrically isolated, can produce pulses up to 100 V at up to 20 mA.

Injury can still occur from careless use of these devices. Several points must be observed for safe operation of the Isolated Stimulator:

1. The Isolated Stimulator output should only be used with the supplied bar stimulus electrode. It must not be used with individual stimulating electrodes. Stimulation must not be applied across the chest or head. Do not hold one electrode in each hand.
2. Always use a suitable electrode cream or gel and proper skin preparation to ensure a low-impedance electrode contact. Using electrodes without electrode paste can result in burns to the skin or discomfort to the subject.
3. Subjects with implantable or external cardiac pacemakers, a cardiac condition, or a history of epileptic episodes should not be subject to electrical stimulation.
4. Always commence stimulation at the lowest current setting and slowly increase the current.
5. Stop stimulation if the subject experiences pain or discomfort.
6. Do not use faulty cables, or those that have exhibited intermittent faults.
7. Always check the status indicator on the front panel. It should always flash green each time the stimulator delivers a current pulse. A yellow flash indicates "out of compliance" condition that may be due to the electrical contact drying up.
8. Always be alert for any signs of adverse physiological effects in the subject. At the first sign of a problem stimulation should be stopped either from the software or by flicking the safety switch on the front of the PowerLab.

McMASTER UNIVERSITY

Complete Policy Title: **POLICY ON THE CARE AND USE OF ANIMALS IN RESEARCH AND TEACHING**

Policy Number (if applicable): **n/a**

Approved by: **Senate**

Date of Most Recent Approval: **November 9, 1994**

Revision Date(s):

Position Responsible for Developing and Maintaining the Policy: **V.P. Research**

Contact Department: **Committee on Scientific Development**

DISCLAIMER: *If there is a discrepancy between this electronic policy and the written copy held by the Policy owner, the written copy prevails.*

McMaster University maintains a policy supporting the responsible use of animals in research for the purpose of obtaining knowledge essential to preventing and curing human and animal disease, eliminating pain and suffering, and in teaching for the purpose of scientific and technical education. McMaster University co-operates and complies with all agencies regulating the use of laboratory animals.

PRINCIPLES OF ANIMAL CARE

The provision of humane care of animals in research and teaching will be assured by adherence to the following principles:

1. All projects involving the use of animals must be approved by the Animal Research Ethics Board in accordance with the regulations of the Animals for Research Act of the Province of Ontario and the guidelines of the Canadian Council on Animal Care.
2. Animals will only be used when alternative procedures are not feasible.
3. The species will be carefully selected to ensure the most effective use of animals.
4. The least invasive techniques possible will be employed.
5. The number of animals used will be the minimum required to achieve the objectives of the research/teaching programme.
6. Alleviation/reduction of pain and distress will be of prime concern during and following all procedures.
7. All animals will be cared for according to current veterinary standards.

OFFICIAL POLICY ON INSTITUTIONAL USE OF ANIMALS

We are a research intensive institution, involving extensive use of animals in biomedical research. Our high ranking in life science research (first in Canada ahead of the University of Toronto and Queen's University) by Science Watch, the newsletter published by the Institute for Scientific Information, is largely due to results from animal experimentation.

We need an official policy for internal and external reasons:

Internal

- to enable the Animal Research Ethics Board and the University Veterinarian to enforce the guidelines of the Canadian Council for Animal Care (necessary for compliance and awarding of grants) and the regulations of the Ontario Ministry of Agriculture and Food (necessary for maintaining an animal facility) with the researchers/users.

External

- to respond to potential challenges from Animal Rights/Welfare groups and to promote positive public relations with the community at large regarding our concern for appropriate care of animals.

Approved by Senate - November 9, 1994

Approved by Combined Operations Grip - May 31, 1994

Approved by Science and Engineering Research Board - April 29, 1993 (in Principle)

Approved by Animal Ethics Commitee - November 5, 1991

Lab 1
Dissection of the Pig Mediastinum

Objective:

The objective of this lab is to identify the different structures of the heart and understand their function.

Keyword List:

Auricles
Atria
Ventricles
Coronary arteries
      Right, left and circumflex
      Anterior Interventricular
      Branch or Left Anterior
      Descending Branch (LAD)
Pulmonary trunk
Aorta
Pericardial sac
Phrenic nerves
Mediastinum
Descending thoracic aorta
Inferior vena cava
Superior vena cava
Intercostals arteries
Esophagus
Vagus nerves
Lymph nodes
Tricuspid valve
Right A/V valve
Bicuspid Valve
Left A/V value
Mitral Valve
Fossa ovalis
Coronary sinus
Cordae tendinae
Papillary muscles
Trabeculae carnae
Pulmonary valve
Semilunar valves

Kin 1AA3/1YY3/2YY3
Lab 1

Safety: If you at any time begin to feel faint or light headed during this lab, please **notify your TA and have a seat on the floor.**

Exercise 1: Overview – Before you begin to dissect

Orient the pluck. The apex of the heart points inferiorly and the opening of the trachea points superiorly. In these specimens the trachea, a cartilaginous tube, often contains froth.

For each of the following:
- identify the structure
- observe location
- consider function

Heart

- observe surface appearance

- identify right and left auricles, atria, ventricles, major coronary arteries, pulmonary trunk and aorta

Is the wall of the pulmonary trunk or the aorta thicker? Why?

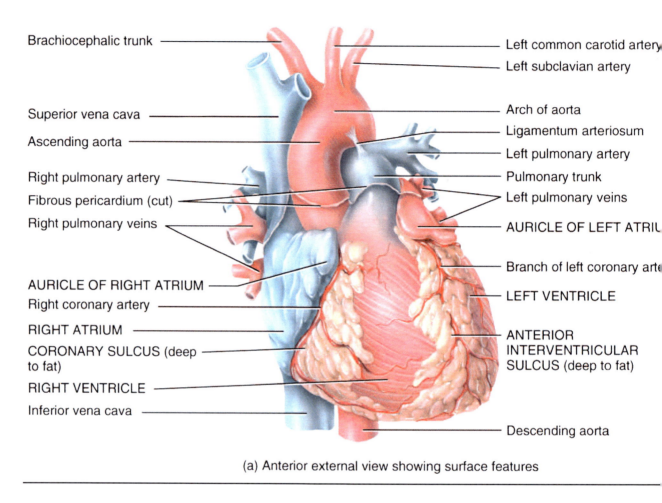

Brachiocephalic trunk

Superior vena cava

Ascending aorta

Right pulmonary artery

Fibrous pericardium (cut)

Right pulmonary veins

AURICLE OF RIGHT ATRIUM

Right coronary artery

RIGHT ATRIUM

CORONARY SULCUS (deep to fat)

RIGHT VENTRICLE

Inferior vena cava

Left common carotid artery

Left subclavian artery

Arch of aorta

Ligamentum arteriosum

Left pulmonary artery

Pulmonary trunk

Left pulmonary veins

AURICLE OF LEFT ATRIUM

Branch of left coronary artery

LEFT VENTRICLE

ANTERIOR INTERVENTRICULAR SULCUS (deep to fat)

Descending aorta

(a) Anterior external view showing surface features

- observe the ring of fat in the coronary sulcus that encircles the heart between the atria and the ventricles. The right and left coronary artery lie embedded in this fat.

- press on the surface of the right and left ventricles and compare their firmness. **Which is firmer? Explain why?**

is thicker
Aorta ↑, blood travels there at a higher pressure
Left ventricle is firmer, needs to circulate blood
in body, has to overcome pressure in entire body

Pericardial sac

- (only part remains on some specimens)
- pull the sides of the sac down so that they enclose the heart. Note the "whitish" phrenic nerve running over the lateral aspects of the sac. Follow the phrenic nerve to where it innervated the diaphragm.

**Does the phrenic nerve carry motor, sensory, or both types of fibers?
From which spinal cord level does the phrenic nerve arise?**

In the pericardial sac

arises from C3 - C5

Both sensory and motor

In humans the pericardial sac is continuous with the diaphragm (the heart moves with each breath) but it is not in pigs due to their different thoracic structure. Note that the diaphragm is a thick white sheet of connective tissue that is edged by skeletal muscle. You should be able to find a hole in the diaphragm that is actually a tube that extends up into the right side of the heart. This is the inferior vena cava (IVC) and is the biggest, thickest vein in the body.

Respiratory tract

- Identify the trachea (feel the horseshoe shaped cartilages in the wall), main bronchi and the lungs (multilobed in pigs).

Why are the cartilages horseshoe shaped?

Food , to allow for swallowing

Mediastinum

- region in thorax that lies between lungs, contains heart, trachea, esophagus, and other vital structures

- identify the ascending aorta, aortic arch, and its branches

- identify the superior vena cava (SVC)

- turn the specimen over to expose the descending thoracic aorta
- cut open the descending aorta and note opening of the intercostals arteries and the smooth inner surface. A healthy human aorta should look like this. **Yours might not? Why?** We have plaque , lots of fat (high fat diet, smoking, & exercise)

 - It is interesting to note that pigs who are kept as pets and fed human food scraps as treats are developing cardiovascular diseases that mimic human diseases

- palpate the firm and lumpy lymph nodes along the aorta (they look like kidney beans)

Exercise 2: Dissection of Heart

Cut heart free from rest of pluck by severing pulmonar
and pulmonary veins.   Hold the heart up away from the rest of the specimen and cut vessels with scissors as far from the surface of the heart as possible.

Examine the chambers and valves by 'following the course of flowing blood'.

Right side:

- Extend an incision through the superior vena cava and through the wall of the right atrium to the tricuspid valve.

- Examine the features of the right atrium: note the smooth walls and try to find the fossa ovalis.

- Examine the interior of right auricle. The interior is lined with bundles of myocardial fibers called pectinate muscles that structurally resemble the interior of the ventricles.

- The right atrioventricular (or tricuspid) valve is located at the bottom of the right atrium. Cusps of the valve appear a whitish flaps.

- The opening of the coronary sinus is just behind the opening of the inferior vena cava. You should be able to insert your little finger into the opening.

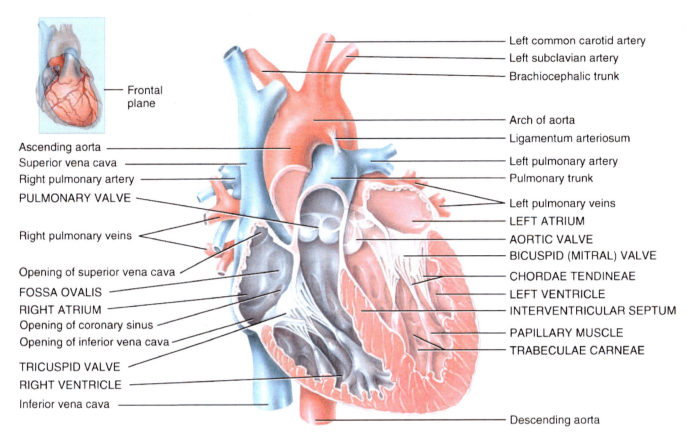

Ascending aorta
Superior vena cava
Right pulmonary artery
PULMONARY VALVE

Right pulmonary veins

Opening of superior vena cava
FOSSA OVALIS
RIGHT ATRIUM
Opening of coronary sinus
Opening of inferior vena cava

TRICUSPID VALVE
RIGHT VENTRICLE
Inferior vena cava

Frontal plane

Left common carotid artery
Left subclavian artery
Brachiocephalic trunk

Arch of aorta
Ligamentum arteriosum
Left pulmonary artery
Pulmonary trunk

Left pulmonary veins
LEFT ATRIUM
AORTIC VALVE
BICUSPID (MITRAL) VALVE
CHORDAE TENDINEAE
LEFT VENTRICLE
INTERVENTRICULAR SEPTUM
PAPILLARY MUSCLE
TRABECULAE CARNEAE

Descending aorta

(a) Anterior view of frontal section showing internal anatomy

Extend incision through the tricuspid valve and the wall of right ventricle towards apex ('pointed' aspect at bottom of ventricles) of the heart. In the ventricle examine: <u>cusps</u>, <u>chordae tendinae</u>, <u>papillary muscles.</u>

What is the of papillary muscles function?

Contract to pull the chordiae tendinea
to close valves

Cusps are the thin white membranes on the superior ends of the white heart strings (chordae tendinae). You should be able to use a glass rod to pull the cusp away from the wall of the ventricle. The papillary muscles are attached to the inferior ends of the chordae tendinae.

Examine wall of the right ventricle. Note thickness (compare with thickness of atria and left ventricle). Note the <u>trabeculae carnae</u>.

Why does a 'wave of depolarization' at one myocardial cell lead to depolarization and contraction of adjacent cells and the entire ventricular myocardium?

Gap junctions
Intercalated disk
desmosomes

What is the name of the pacemaker of the heart?

SA Node

Extend incision up through <u>pulmonary valve</u> and into <u>pulmonary trunk</u>. Examine pulmonary valve (three <u>'semilunar' cusps</u>) consider the forces that cause this valve to open and close. **Compare with the other valves**.

Left side:

Follow similar procedure as for the right side. Extend an incision from the top of the left atrium, through the bicuspid valve, and to the ottom of the left ventricle. Identify structures and compare and contrast the valves and wall thickness to the right side
Compare and contrast sides

Locate and probe <u>right and left coronary arteries</u> that arise from behind cusps of aortic valve. The openings of the coronary arteries are behind and above the cusps of the aortic semilunar valves. The coronary arteries fill during diastole when the heart muscle is relaxed.

Case Study/Pathology

Arjun was born in India and moved to Canada with his family when he was 10. Arjun is now 17 and has begun playing soccer at his high school. Arjun has noticed after the last few practices where the team did a lot of running, he was short of breath. He has also been unusually tired. Arjun visits his doctor who listens to his heart and suspects a heart murmur. An echocardiogram reveals that Arjun has mitral valve stenosis.

Examine specimen CV-2-S3 and identify the chambers and the mitral valve prosthesis

Describe how this prosthesis would function.

A ball in the place of valve

left atrium pressure > left ventricle, ball moves down
left atrium pressure < left ventricle, ball moves up and blocks

What would happen if mitral valve stenosis is left untreated?

Backflow → less blood in Systemic circulation

May cause blood in alveoli from increased pressure in left ventricle

Summary of Questions:

Is the wall of the pulmonary trunk or the aorta thicker? Why?

After pressing on the surface of the right and left ventricles which is firmer? Explain why?

Does the phrenic nerve carry motor, sensory, or both types of fibers? From which spinal cord level does the phrenic nerve arise?

Why are the cartilages of the trachea horseshoe shaped?

Why might the inside of your aorta not be as smooth as the pig aorta?

What is the of papillary muscles function?

Why does a 'wave of depolarization' at one myocardial cell lead to depolarization and contraction of adjacent cells and the entire ventricular myocardium?

What is the name of the pacemaker of the heart?

Compare and contrast the semilunar valves and atrioventricular valves.

Compare and contrast the right and left ventricles.

Lab 2

Cardiovascular Physiology and Blood Analysis

Objectives

It is important to gain an understanding of the relationship of the clinical measures of cardiac function to the anatomy and physiology of the circulatory system. The objective of this lab is to experiment with the methods of measuring pulse, blood pressure, and the heart's electrical activity to gain an understanding how each measure relates to cardiovascular function. You will utilize both the traditional methods and the Lab Tutor.

In today's lab you will use Lab Tutor to examine the electrical activity of the heart through an electrocardiogram (ECG) and record this together with the pulse and heart sounds. You will gain an appreciation for how the electrical events of the heart correlate with the other measures of cardiovascular function. Thus, in this experiment, you will be able to examine the relationship between the timing of the electrocardiogram and the pulsatile flow of blood.

Again using Lab Tutor, you will become familiar with measuring the blood pressure of volunteers. The traditional method using a pressure cuff with a sphygmomanometer and a stethoscope will be compared with using Lab Tutor to observe the changes in blood flow using pulse measurement to replace the stethoscope, while measuring blood pressure.

You will also have the unique opportunity to determine your blood type and hematocrit.

Background – Please read this information BEFORE attending lab

The heart is a dual pump that pushes blood around the body and through the lungs. Blood enters the atrial chambers of the heart at a low pressure and leaves the ventricles at a higher pressure; it is this high arterial pressure that provides the energy to force blood through the circulatory system. Figure 1 shows the organization of the human heart and the circulatory system, in schematic form. Blood returning from the body arrives at the right side of the heart and is pumped through the lungs to pick up oxygen and release carbon dioxide. This oxygenated blood then arrives at the left side of the heart, from where it is pumped back to the body.

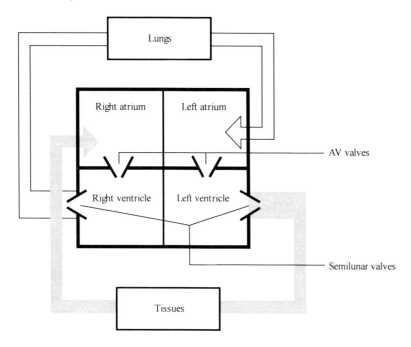

Figure 1. A schematic diagram of the human heart and circulatory system.

Cardiac contractions are not dependent upon a nerve supply. A group of specialized muscle cells (sinoatrial or sinuatrial node, SA node) acts as the pacemaker for the heart (Figure 2). These cells rhythmically produce action potentials that spread through the fibers of the atria. The resulting contraction pushes blood into the ventricles. The only electrical connection between the atria and the ventricles is via the atrioventricular (AV) node. The action potential spreads slowly through the AV node (thus giving a time delay for ventricular filling) and then rapidly through the AV bundle and Purkinje fibers to excite both ventricles. The large muscle mass of the ventricles allows powerful contractions.

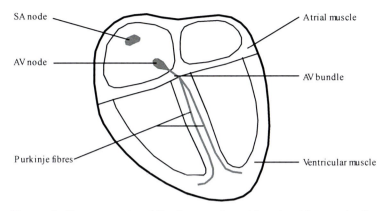

Figure 2. Components of the human heart involved in conduction.

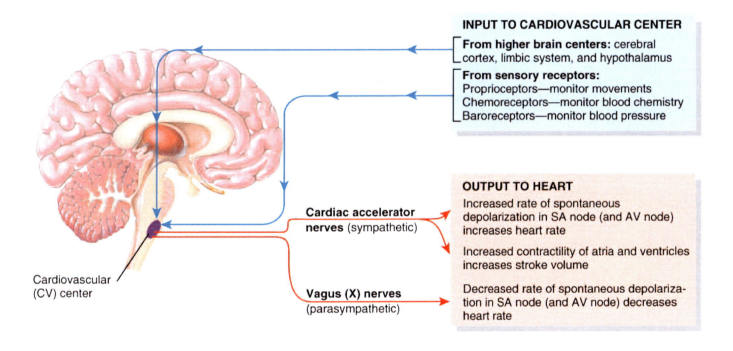

Figure 3 shows the innervation of the heart by the autonomic nervous system.

Each side of the heart is provided with two valves, to convert rhythmic contractions into a unidirectional pumping. The valves close automatically whenever there is a pressure difference across the valve that would cause backflow of blood. Closure gives rise to audible vibrations (heart sounds). The right and left Atrioventricular (AV) valves between the atrium and ventricle on each side of the heart prevent backflow from ventricle to atrium.
What are other names for these valves?

Semilunar valves are located between the ventricle and the artery on each side of the heart, and prevent backflow of blood from artery to ventricle. **What are their names?**

The cardiac cycle involves a sequential contraction of the atria and the ventricles. The combined electrical activity of the different myocardial cells produces electrical currents that spread through the body fluids. These currents are large enough to be detected by recording electrodes placed on the skin. The regular pattern of peaks produced by each heart beat cycle is called the electrocardiogram or ECG (Figure 4).

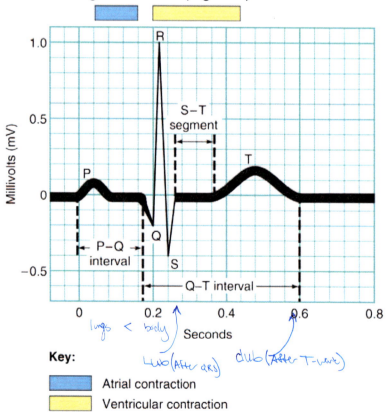

Key:

Atrial contraction

Ventricular contraction

Figure 4. A typical ECG showing the fundamental parts of the signal.

The action potentials recorded from atrial and ventricular fibers are different from those recorded from nerves and skeletal muscle. *Remember that the skeletal muscle activity was recorded by EMG and that it looked like a series of irregular spikes. Myocardial activity is much more consistent and more regulated than skeletal muscle action potentials.* The cardiac action potential is composed of three phases: a rapid depolarization, a plateau depolarization (which is very obvious in ventricular fibers), and a repolarization back to resting membrane potential.

The components of the ECG can be correlated with the electrical activity of the atrial and ventricular muscle:

- the P-wave is produced by atrial depolarization
- the QRS complex is produced by ventricular depolarization; atrial repolarization also occurs during this time
- the T-wave is produced by ventricular repolarization.

The characteristic sound produced by the heart is usually referred to as a 'lub-dup' sound. The lower-pitched 'lub' sound occurs during the early phase of ventricular contraction and is produced by closing of the atrioventricular valves (the mitral valve and tricuspid valve), which prevent blood from flowing back into the atria. When the ventricles relax, the blood pressure drops below that in the artery and the semilunar valves (aortic and pulmonary) close, producing the higher-pitched 'dup' sound.

greatest variability from the P to the T-wave between different people.

The pressure in the arteries varies during the cardiac cycle. The ventricles contract to push blood into the arterial system and then relax to fill with blood before pumping once more. This intermittent ejection of blood into the arteries is balanced by a constant loss of blood from the arterial system through the capillaries. When the heart pushes blood into the arteries there is a sudden increase in pressure, which slowly declines until the heart contracts again. Blood pressure is at its highest immediately after the ventricle contracts (systolic pressure) and at its lowest immediately prior to the pumping of blood into the arteries (diastolic pressure). Figure 5 demonstrates the relationship among the ECG, volume of blood in the ventricles, blood pressure and the configuration of the heart valves. **When do you hear the heart sounds?**

Low HR → High Stroke Volume

Lub: AV valves closing, blood ventricle contracts

dub: Semilunar valves closing ventricles relax

When would a pulse arrive in your finger as compared to the timing of the heart sounds?

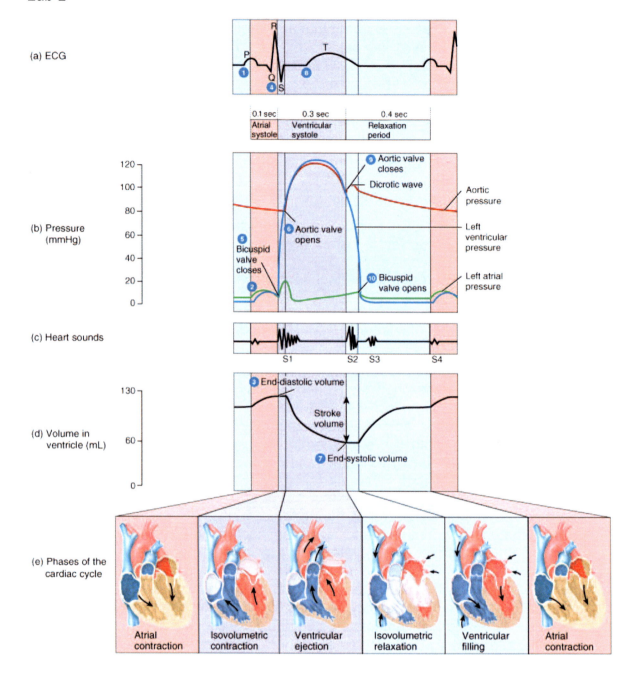

Figure 5 Relationship among ECG, blood volume, blood pressure and the configuration of heart valves.

Systolic and diastolic pressures can be measured by inserting a small catheter into an artery and attaching the catheter to a pressure gauge. Such a direct measurement might be accurate, but is invasive and often inconvenient and impractical. Simpler estimates of blood pressure can be made with acceptable accuracy using noninvasive, indirect methods.

Traditionally, systemic arterial blood pressure is estimated using a stethoscope and a blood pressure cuff connected to a sphygmomanometer (mercury column or otherwise) (Figure 6). The cuff is placed on the upper arm and inflated to stop arterial blood flow to the arm (from the brachial artery); the cuff creates a high pressure that causes the artery to collapse. The pressure in the cuff is released slowly, and when the systolic pressure in the artery is greater than that in the cuff, blood flows momentarily to the arm through the partially collapsed artery. This can be heard through the stethoscope as sharp, tapping sounds (Korotkoff sounds), at which stage cuff pressure is taken to approximate systolic pressure. As cuff pressure is reduced, the sounds heard through the stethoscope increase in intensity and then suddenly become muffled. Cuff pressure at the point of sound muffling is taken to approximate diastolic blood pressure. As cuff pressure is further reduced, the sounds disappear completely, and normal flow through the artery is re-established. Since the disappearance of sound is easier to detect than muffling, and since the two occur within a few millimeters of mercury pressure, the disappearance of sound is commonly used to determine diastolic pressure.

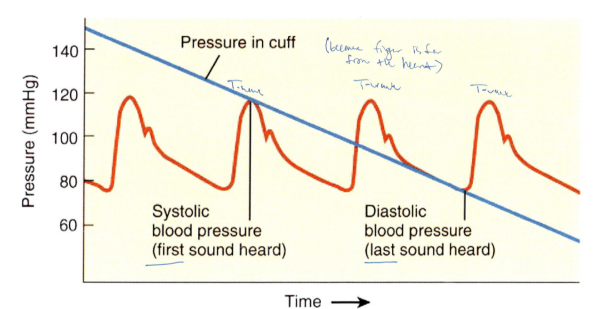

Figure 6 Relationship between blood pressure and the Korotkoff sounds.

If measured closer to the heart, the peak will be closer to the QRS complex as it is near the heart

Korotkoff : Turbulent flow hitting the artery

Station One: Lab Tutor - ECG, Heart Sounds, and Pulse

-Please access lab Tutor on the desktop

-open the Lab Tutor experiment called **ECG, Heart Sounds, and Pulse**

Below are a few sample tracings from Lab Tutor:

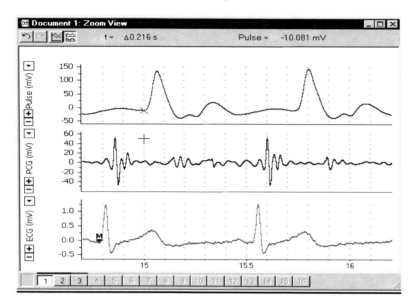

-sample tracing of ECG, PCG, and pulse

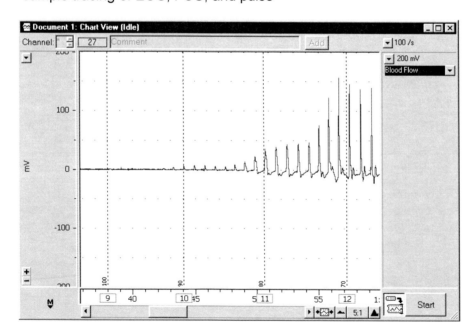

- sample tracing of using Lab Tutor to determine blood pressure

Case Study/Pathology

Brent is a 69 year old sedentary male with a history of cardiovascular disease. One evening after dinner with his wife, Brent says he feel nauseous and sweaty. Within a few minutes, Brent is clearly in distress and is stating he has tightness in his chest and back. His wife calls and ambulance and he is rushed to the Hamilton General. An ECG is performed and the trace looks as follows:

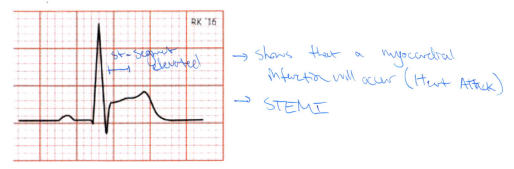

ST-Segment Elevated

→ Shows that a myocardial infarction will occur (Heart Attack)
→ STEMI

Compare and contrast this trace with what you observed during your ECG on the LabTutor

What do you think Brent is suffering from?

STEMI

STEMI at the left descending artery that feeds the left ventricle.

(also called widowmaker)

Station Two: Blood Typing and Hematocrit

Safety: If you at any time begin to feel faint or light headed during this lab, please **notify your TA and have a seat on the floor.**

SAFETY ALERT
FACULTY OF HEALTH SCIENCES McMASTER UNIVERSITY

Universal Precautions Applying to Blood, Bodily Fluids and Tissues
1. Gloves, lab coats and protective eyewear must be worn when coming in contact with blood or bodily fluids.
2. Wash hands when contaminated or immediately after gloves are removed.
3. Take precautions to avoid injuries with sharp instruments.
4. Use only mechanical pipetting devices.
5. Decontaminate work surfaces daily and after spills. Use 1 in 10 household bleach, 70% ethanol, or alternative germicide
6. Remove all lab coats or other protective equipment before leaving the lab

Exercise 1: Blood Typing

The surfaces of red blood cells have molecules called **antigens** and in the plasma, molecules called **antibodies** are present. Antibodies are very specific, meaning that each antibody can only combine with a certain antigen. When the antibodies in the plasma bind to foreign antigens on the surface of RBC's, they form molecular bridges that connect RBC's. As a result, **agglutination**, or clumping, of the RBC's occurs.

The antigens on the surfaces of the RBC's have been classified into blood groups. Over 35 different blood groups exist but today we will look at the ABO blood group. Each blood type has a specific antigen and antibody associated with it:

Type A: A antigens, anti-B antibodies

Type B: B antigens, anti-A antibodies

Type AB: both A and B antigens, neither anti-A or anti-B antibodies

Type O: neither A or B antigrens, both anti-A and anti-B antibodies

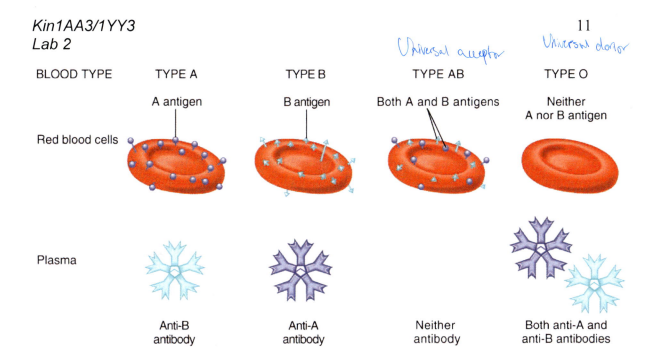

Universal acceptor   Universal donor

Figure 17 – ABO blood groups

In this exercise you will have the opportunity to determine which blood type you have. We will do this by adding **anti-A and anti-B antibody** to your blood and watching for the type of **agglutination** reaction happens.

Safety:

This portion of the lab will involve taking blood samples from a fingertip. If you are sensitive to the sight of blood, you may step back and not participate. Please draw and handle only your OWN blood and wear gloves at all times. All lancets and anything that came into contact with blood should immediately be placed in the YELLOW SHARPS container and the workbench should be washed with Dettol solution. All alcohol swaps and wrappers etc. can go into the regular garbage.

Procedure:

1.   Obtain gloves, toothpick, a sterile lancet, alcohol swab, a tile well and a bottle of anti-A and anti-B antibody from the front bench. Please wear safety glasses.

2.   Before pricking your finger, hold you arm down and try to wave it around. This will hopefully increase the amount of blood in your fingertip.

3.   Take an alcohol swap and run over the fingertip you will be pricking.

4. Using the auto lancets, twist off the protective cap over the needle, place it over your finger and push the end. Place two drops of blood in each of the clean tile wells. Discard in sharps container.

5. Add a drop of anti-A antibody to one well and a drop of anti-B antibody to the other well. Mix each with a toothpick and discard toothpick in sharps container

6. Rock and rotate the tile slowly

Record the presence of agglutination in any of the wells below.

-------------------------	Anti-A antibody	Anti-B antibody
Agglutination	yes	yes

Based on the results you have obtained and what you know about agglutination reactions determine which blood type you have.

Student should now understand how the agglutination reaction will work. Given what they know about the antigens and antibodies present on each blood type they should be able to figure out their blood type based on the reaction in the 2 tile wells.

Type A blood – the well that had anti-A antibody added WILL AGGLUTINATE, well with anti-B antibody will do nothing. WHY? The anti-A antibodies are reacting with the A antigens = agglunation

Type B blood – the well that had anti-B antibody added WILL AGGLUTINATE, well with anti-A antibody added will do nothing. WHY? The anti-B antibody is reacting with the B antigens = agglutination

Type AB blood –BOTH wells will agglutinate. WHY? AB has both antigens therefore both the anti-A and anti-B antibodies will be reacting with an anitgen

Type O blood – NEITHER wells will agglutinate. WHY? O blood has no antigens, therefore there is nothing for the anti-A or anti-B antibody to react with.

Place used tile wells into tub containing bleach and water.

Exercise 2: Hematocrit

The percentage of total blood volume composed of RBC's is the hematocrit. One way to determine hematocrit (and the method we will use today) is to place blood in a tube and spin the tube in a centrifuge. The formed elements (RBC's) are heavier than the plasma and are forced to one end of the tube. White blood cells and platlets form a thin whitish layer, called the buffy coat, between the RBC's and the plasma.

Normal hematocrit for males: 40-54%

Normal hematocrit for females 38-47%

Measuring hemoatocrits can be used to evaluate anemia (low % of RBC's) and polycythemia which is an increase in red blood cells (as seen after being at altitude.)

Procedure:

1. Obtain a drop of blood from a finger with a lancet as done previously and dispose lancet in sharps container.

2. Touch the end of the capillary tube to the blood sample on your finger. To make this easier, hold the tube at less than a 45^0 angle. Stop filling the tube when it is 1cm from the top

3. Hold the tube horizontally and plug the dry end with sealant.

4. Give the sealed tubes to your TA. The tubes will be spun in a hematocrit centrifuge for 1 minute.
5. Measure the height of the dark RBC's and the height of the entire column, or use the hematocrit reader. Dispose capillary into sharps.

Hematocrit = height of RBC's / total height of fluid column

Gender difference

females → Menstrual Cycle
          Body size

hematocrit → more RBC for carry oxygen
          (for athletes)

Lab 3
Respiratory System

[handwritten margin notes: C thyroid muscles → raise / Thyro-cricothyroid muscle → relax]

Objective:

The objective of this lab is to examine the anatomy and physiology of the respiratory system. You will have a chance to look at specimens of the lungs as well as the accessory structures associated with breathing. We will use the Lab Tutor to examine respiratory variables at rest and with forced breathing. You should gain an understanding of the terms used to assess lung functions, their relation to ventilation and respiratory physiology and how these assessments relate to clinical assessment in patients with respiratory difficulties. Finally, using a patient simulator, you will have an opportunity to hear both normal and abnormal (pathological) breath sounds.

Station 1: Respiratory Anatomy

Use the following specimens to examine respiratory anatomy:

Block Specimens:

RP0 772   Larynx: Note the epiglottis and how it can move to seal off the trachea during swallowing. The trachea is opened posteriorly and the c-shaped cartilaginous rings are evident. Note where the hyoid bone has been cut, and the thyrohyoid muscles stretch from this to the thyroid cartilage inferiorly. The thyroid gland itself has been removed. *[margin: Larynx moves up when swallow to block airway]*
(Epiglottis, trachea opened, thyroid cartilage, obscured view of vocal folds.) *Cervical*

RP0 729   Casting of bronchial tree: This casting has the regions supplying *[handwritten: hyoid is connected to the tongue, not articulated with others]* bronchopulmonary segments coloured and numbered. These are, for the most part, tertiary divisions, and are still supported by cartilaginous plates embedded in the bronchial wall. The numbers refer to the following segments.
1) Trachea
2) Segments of Superior Lobe (right) *blue*
3) Segments of Middle Lobe (right) *yellow green*
4) Segments of Inferior Lobe (right) *red*
5) Apical posterior & anterior segments of Superior Lobe (left) *dark green*
6) Superior & Inferior lingular segments of Superior Lobe (left) *yellow*
7) Lower segmental bronchi (left) *dark red*

RP0 809   Left Lung: The hilum of the lung is the region where the structures supplying the lung with blood and with air enter the soft tissue of the organ itself. Note the relationships between the Pulmonary artery, veins, and the primary bronchus. Refer to the plastic model with the transparent lungs to gain a full appreciation of the relationships between the structures. The lung will receive impressions from mediastinal contents pressed up against it.

RP1 1501   Diaphragm: The diaphragm is a muscular sheet with a central disc of tendon that acts as a seal between the thoracic and abdominal cavities. Three structures pass through the diaphragm. Two leave distinct openings, listed below. What is the third?
(Central tendon, esophageal hiatus, claval opening (for IVC), crus of diaphragm,) *Central tendon attached to the lungs*

Wet Specimens: *passes → esophagus, inferior vena cava, descending aorta*

Left and Right Lungs: hilum (pulmonary artery, veins, primary bronchus), lobes (3 in right, 2 in left)

Mediastinum: The term mediastinum refers to a division between two parts of an organ or cavity. In this case it refers to the central mass of heart *Cardiac notch on left* and associated blood vessels separating the thoracic cavity. This specimen has latex infused into the pericardium, surrounding and obscuring the heart within. The right lung of this specimen only has 2 of the three lobes apparent.

Identify the Pericardium, Thoracic aorta, Aortic arch (branches: brachiocephalic trunk, left common carotid, left subclavian, pulmonary trunk.)

Case Study/Pathology

Jerry worked as a Fire Captain in Hamilton for over 35 years. After retirement he noticed he was began to feel unusually out of breath after walking up stairs or jogging to catch the bus. Over time, he began to notice that even walking around his home was leaving him gasping for air.

Examine specimen RP2 741

Hold the specimen up to the light and report what you see.

Assume this is a specimen similar to Jerry's lung, what do you think he is suffering from? *Emphysema (COPD, death of alveoli) exposed to smoke, Alveoli burst, lack of area for gas exchange.*

Other Pathologies:

RP2 169   Carcinoma of the lung: This specimen has extensive carbon deposits evident in the tissue of the lung. Between the two lungs is a massive central tumour with esophagus and trachea embedded.

Station 2 - Spirometry

You will use Lab Tutor to take readings on Tidal Volume (**V_T**), Inspiratory Reserve Volume (IRV), Expiratory Reserve Volume (ERV), Forced Expired Volume in one second (FEV$_1$**)** and calculate Vital Capacity (VC). You may then compare for example a smoker vs. non-smoker, those who exercise vs. couch potatoes, boys vs. girls and perhaps those who have allergies or asthma vs. healthy subjects. This should be interesting and fun.

Background

Gas exchange between air and blood occurs in the alveolar air sacs. The efficiency of gas exchange is dependent on ventilation: cyclical breathing movements that alternately inflate and deflate the volume of the alveolar air sacs. Inspiration refills the alveoli with fresh atmospheric air and expiration removes stale air, which has reduced oxygen and increased carbon dioxide concentrations.

Spirometry is becoming more and more important, as respiratory diseases are increasing word wide. Spirometry is the method of choice for a fast and reliable screening of patients suspected of having Chronic Obstructive Pulmonary Disease (COPD). COPD is the 12th leading cause of death worldwide and the 5th leading cause in Western countries. Studies suggest COPD could climb to be the 3rd leading killer by 2020. Most COPD cases are completely avoidable; 85-90% of cases are caused by tobacco smoking.

Spirometry allows many components of pulmonary function (as shown in Figure 1) to be visualized, measured and calculated. Respiration consists of repeating cycles of inspiration followed by expiration. During the respiratory cycle, a specific volume of air is drawn into and then expired out of the lungs; this volume is the **Tidal Volume (V_T)**. In normal ventilation, the breathing frequency (f) is approximately 15 respiratory cycles per minute. This value varies with the level of activity. The product of f and V_T is the Expired Minute Volume (V_E), the amount of air exhaled in one minute of breathing. This parameter also changes according to the level of activity.

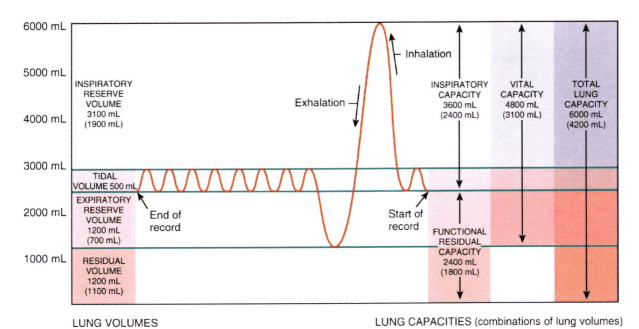

Figure 1. Lung volumes and capacities.

Forced parameters, which assess the ability to ventilate the lungs with maximal voluntary effort, are often of greater clinical value than simple lung volumes and capacities. Forced Expired Volume in one second (FEV1), Peak Inspiratory Flow (PIF) and Peak Expiratory Flow (PEF) are strongly affected by airway resistance, and are important in the detection and monitoring of obstructive disorders (bronchitis, emphysema and asthma).

Forced Vital Capacity (FVC) is similar to VC, but is obtained from measurement of a single expiration; it is reduced in restrictive disorders such as pulmonary fibrosis. The FVC is graphically represented as larger than VC in theory, but the FVC is often smaller than the VC in practice. The total capacity of the lungs is comprised of four functionally separate lung volumes: Tidal Volume (V_T), Inspiratory Reserve Volume (IRV), Expiratory Reserve Volume (ERV) and Residual Volume (RV).

Procedure: **Start Lab Tutor on your desktop**

- You take up your results with your group. What did you find?
- Was there a difference between exercisers and sedentary people with any of the measures?
- Was there a difference between people with lung disorders and otherwise healthy people? Lower flow, less efficient
- Can you explain the difference between obstructive and restrictive lung disease. → something in your airways vs. restricting lungs to expand (lowers lung capacity)

caused by
Mostly lifestyle choices, not as much of environment/genetics.

Below are some sample tracings from Lab Tutor:

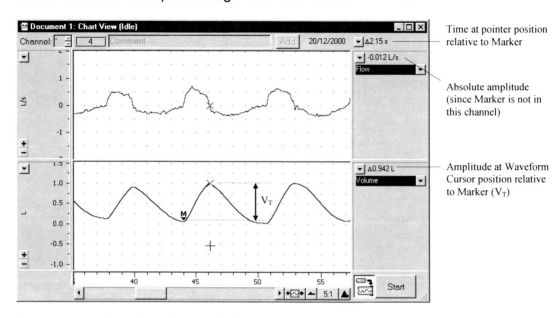

Figure 2. A typical tidal breathing record, displayed at 5:1 horizontal compression. The Marker and Waveform Cursor are positioned to measure the Tidal Volume of a single breath.

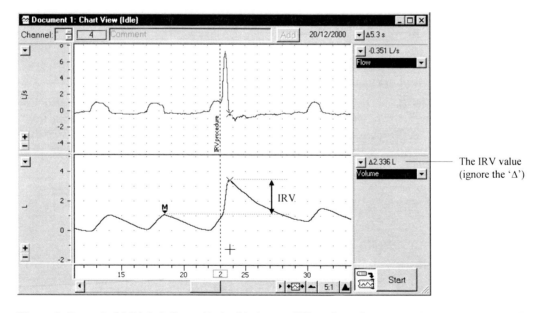

Figure 3. Record of full inhalation, with the Marker and Waveform Cursor positioned to measure IRV.

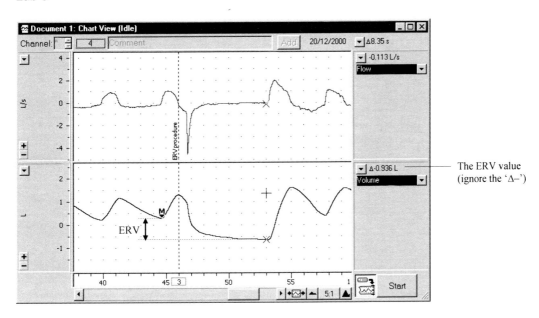

Figure 4. Record of full exhalation, with the Marker and Waveform Cursor positioned to measure ERV.

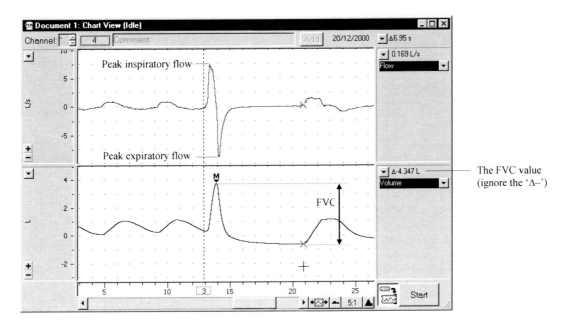

Figure 5. A spirometry recording showing where to find PIF and PEF, and how to determine FVC.

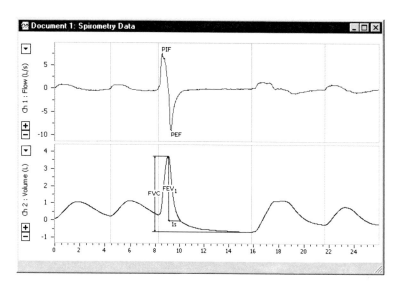

Figure 6. The Spirometry Data window, with the locations of the forced expiration parameters indicated.

Station 3 – VitalSim Patient Simulator

The VitalSim is patient simulator that is used in a variety of teaching settings. We will be using them throughout the term to teach components of the cardiovascular and respiratory systems.

Objective:
- To become familiar with the basic operation and correct use of the VitalSim.
- To asses both heart rate and respiratory rate.
- To gain appreciation for the difference between normal and abnormal breath sounds

Equipment:
Laerdal VitalSim Remote
VitalSim Vital Signs Stimulator Box
Annie (the simulated patient)
Stopwatch or timer on computer

Instructions:

Turning the system ON
1. Press the large green button on the Vital Signs Simulator Box. The green light should now be blinking.
2. Press the POWER button on the remote control located in the bottom left corner. A solid green light should now appear on the Vital Signs Simulator Box.

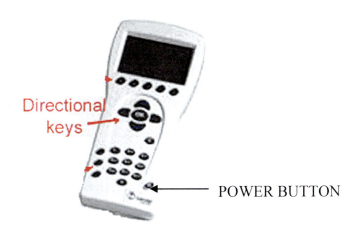

Directional keys

POWER BUTTON

The VitalSim system can be set up to simulate many normal and pathological states. Breathing rate, heart rate, ECG rhythm, breathing sounds, and heart sounds are only a few of the parameters that can be altered with this system.

Navigating the Menu:

A menu screen should now appear on the VitalSim remote. You will notice that the screen is split into two halves. The left side control cardiovascular parameters while the right side control breathing and heat sounds. Today we will be focusing on the heart rate and breathing settings only.

Heart Rate

> Your TA will program the heart rate settings into the VitalSim and it is up to you to correctly assess you patient.

> 1. You are now ready to check Annie's radial pulse.
> 2. You will place two fingers over Annie's radial pulse
>   NOTE: The amount of pressure you apply when taking the pulse is key. The pulse is generated by an electrical device that is sensitive to pressure. Too much pressure and no pulse will be felt as the "blood flow will be occluded". Too little pressure and the pulse will not be felt.
> 3. Record the pulse for 10 seconds and then figure out beats per minute (multiply the 10 second count by 6).

Breathing

The **respiratory rate** is the number of breaths a person takes within a certain amount of time (frequently given in breaths per minute). The average respiratory rate reported in a healthy adult at rest is usually given as around 12 breaths per minute. This can be higher or lower in different pathological states.

Breath sounds refer to the specific sounds identified through auscultation of the respiratory system with a stethoscope

Your TA will program the settings into the VitalSim and it is up to you to correctly assess you patient.

> 1. Obtain one of the stethoscopes and you are now ready to assess Annie's breathing rate.

2. An examination done by a physician would be much more thorough than what we will do today. They would be sure to auscultate the apices and middle and lower lung fields posteriorly, laterally and anteriorly. They would then repeat this on the alternate lung and compare sides.

3. Place the stethoscope over the apex of the lung (inferior to the clavicle). Keeping an eye on the clock, count how many breaths Annie takes in 1 minute. You could also auscultate at the base of the lungs (lateral to the midline at the level of the xiphoid process.

In addition to assessing respiratory rate, you can also listen to a variety of breath sounds.

Your TA will program in some different breath sounds for you to hear. You can auscultate the lungs in the same manner that you did when you assess respiratory rate.

Wheeze → Continuous, coarse, whistling sound produced in airways. Increased air velocity in respiratory tree. Caused by constant tidal volume travelling through narrow airway. Ex. Asthma

Stridor → Type of wheeze caused by obstructed upper airway. Tracheal/Laryngeal obstruction. Allergic reaction or tracheal obstruction. Expiration → lower blockage, Inspiration → upper blockage above carina. (Most audible)

Pneumonia Crackles → Lung tissue undergoes inflammation and alveoli fill with fluid. Lungs sound deeper and more hollow sanding. Crumpling of candy wrapper at the end of inspiration. High respiration rate. (end of inspiration)

Rhonchi → coarse rattling sound heard during exhalation. Due to production of mucous secretions, bronchospasm. Associated with COPD and bronchitis.

Pleural Rub → Visceral and Parietal pleura become inflamed. Crackling/Rubbing sound. Short inspiration as it is painful. Low breathing rate

D Crackles Pneumonia → Mucous of fluid collects in the distal part of the lungs causing alveoli to collapse. During inspiration, alveoli pop open and create crackling sound of burning wood, Tidal volume is increased.

Lab 4
Gastrointestinal Anatomy

Objective:
To introduce the regions of the gastrointestinal system, describe the organs and their functions.

Keyword List:

Oro/Nasopharnynx:
Parotid gland
Submandibular gland
Esophagus Palate
Masseter muscle
Uvula
Epiglottis

Small Intestine:
Duodenum
Jejunum
Ileum
Lumen
Chymotrypsinogen
Trypsinogen
Procarboxypeptidase
Membrane-bound
Entrokinase
Plicae circularis
Ampulla of Vater (hepatopancreatic sphincter)
Mesentery
Villi
Microvilli

Pancreas:
Pancreatic duct

Large Intestine:
Ascending Colon
Cecum
Appendix
Transverse Colon
Descending Colon
Sigmoid Colon
Rectum

Anus

Stomach:
Mucus
Fundus
Esophageal sphincter
Chyme
Rugae
Antrum
Pylorus
Pyloric sphincter
HCl
Intrinsic
Pepsinogen
Gastrin
Mesocolin
Teniae Coli
Haustra
Epiploic appendage

Liver:
Common Bile duct
Ileocecal valve
Ligamentum teres
Falicform ligament
Hepatic portal system
Gallbladder

Arteries:
Celiac trunk
    Left gastric
    Splenic
    Hepatic arteries
Mesenteric arteries

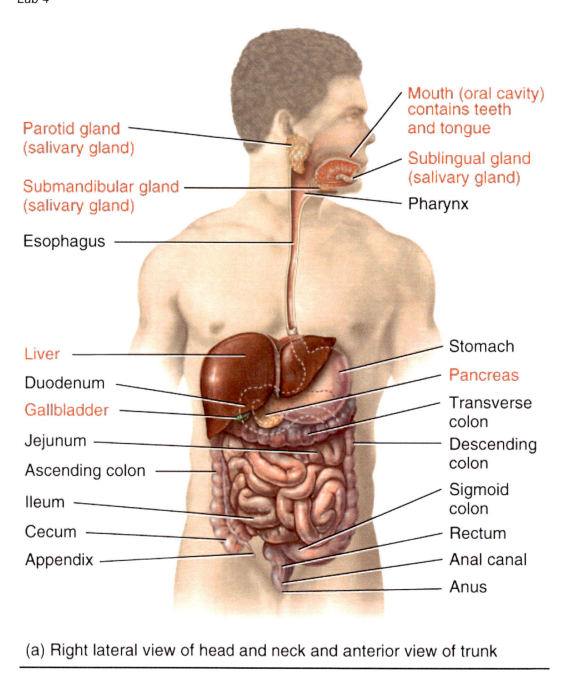

Parotid gland
(salivary gland)

Submandibular gland
(salivary gland)

Esophagus

Mouth (oral cavity)
contains teeth
and tongue

Sublingual gland
(salivary gland)

Pharynx

Liver

Duodenum

Gallbladder

Jejunum

Ascending colon

Ileum

Cecum

Appendix

Stomach

Pancreas

Transverse
colon

Descending
colon

Sigmoid
colon

Rectum

Anal canal

Anus

(a) Right lateral view of head and neck and anterior view of trunk

Figure 1. Organs of the digestive tract.

Station One

Exericse One: Oro/Nasopharynx

mastication + saliva

The nasopharynx is the superior portion of the pharynx and is separated from the oral cavity by the soft palate. It is lined by typical respiratory epithelium. The lateral walls contain the openings of the auditory tubes. The oropharynx extends from the soft palate and the base of the tongue; it is lined with stratified squamous epithelium. The laryngopharynx is the most inferior part of the pharynx.

Examine **HN10(1),** a plastic head model showing the masseter muscle which elevates the mandible. This muscle can be felt by clenching your teeth and feeling along the jaw bone. The temporalis muscle is not present but would be superior to the ear, covering the temple region. This is the muscle that gets sore when chewing stale bubblegum. The pterygoids lie underneath the masseter muscle and cannot be seen in this model.

Specimen **HN6S4** shows the submandibular gland. The ducts for this gland enter the oral cavity underneath the tongue (on either side of the lingual frenulum). Students may be able to see these tiny openings underneath their own tonges in a mirror. A small portion of the parotid gland can be seen in this specimen.

The parotid gland is better seen in specimen **HN6S5.** The parotid gland empties near the 2nd molars, and these openings can actually be felt with your own tongue.

muscle

hard palate → bone

Observe model **JS2/2** which demonstrates the pathways of the oropharynx that are shared between the digestive and respiratory tracts. **Can you identify the soft palate, uvula and epiglottis? What structures must be blocked off to ensure swallowed food enters the esophagus?**

cartilage

bones nasal cavity

*nasopharynx
↓
oropharynx
↓
laryngopharynx*

Exericse Two: Esophagus

The esophagus is approximately 25 cm long and connects the pharynx to the stomach. About 5 cm is in the neck region, 2 cm is termed the abdominal esophagus and the rest is the thoracic esophagus. The esophagus can be opacified by barium and visualized on radiography. The left atrium lies in front of the esophagus **(GI3C1)** and thus enlargement of this compartment can be visualized by a compressed esophagus.

*neck 5 cm
↓
thoracic 25 cm
↓
abdominal 2 cm*

Observe specimen **GI3S2** and note the relative positions of the esophagus and aorta. The lower esophageal sphincter **(GI3S1-radiograph)** at the diaphragm causes the food bolus to "pause" before entering the stomach, and this expanded region of the esophagus (seen in some of the radiographs) is called the phrenic ampulla. The opening in the diaphragm that permits the passing of the esophagus is called the <u>esophageal hiatus.</u> Inflammation usually occurs when acid cannot be held down by the sphincter, thus burning the inside of the esophagus (and giving the condition known as 'heart burn')

acid going from Stomach to the esophagus and burns the wall

Exercise Three: Stomach

The stomach is mainly a storage area along the digestive tract which regulates the ejection of acidic chyme through the pyloric sphincter (pyloric-duodenal juncture) and into the duodenum. The empty stomach has a capacity of 50 mL and the inner walls consist of deep folds called **rugae**. Once the 50 ml capacity of the stomach is exceeded, the stomach begins to expand and the rugae flatten out. The maximum capacity of the stomach is 1-1.5 L. A hiatus hernia occurs when the stomach slips up through the esophageal hiatus (where the esophagus penetrates the diaphragm) as a result of the weakening of the connective tissues around the gastro-esophageal juncture. Simple columnar epithelium covers the entire stomach

Observe specimen **GI4S2 (McM 435)**. The fundus of the stomach is above the entry point of the esophagus into the stomach. The pyloric region is the region around the pyloric sphincter and the body makes up the majority of the stomach.

What are the folds in the stomach interior called?

Observe the specimen **GI4S4**, this stomach has been expanded to capacity.

What has happened to the folds?

Observe specimen **GI 4S3** and identify the following features:

- Fundus
- Body
- Pyloric part
- Esophageal hiatus
- Pyloric sphincter → *bottom sphincter*
- Lesser and Greater Curvatures
-

The fundus and body have gastric pits that extend down into gastric glands for the secretion of gastric fluid.

What are the components of the gastric fluids?

Hydrochloric acid
Pepsinogen
Intrinsic factor, → helps absorption of B12
Gastric lipase
Mucus.

Simple Columnar.

Station Two

Exercise One: Duodenum and Pancreas

The duodenum is the first part of the small intestine and begins at the pyloric sphincter. The duodenum is retroperitoneal (lies mostly on the posterior abdominal wall behind the peritoneum) but the first portion of the duodenum is visible in the torso as a c-shaped loop which surrounds the pancreas. The first 2.5 cm of the duodenum is small walled and has a flat interior but the rest contains numerous circular folds called plicae circularis which increase the surface area of the small intestine. The folds decrease in density and height as you progress from the duodenum through the jejunum and finally to the ileum. Look at specimen **GI6S5** which is a longitudinal section of the duodenum and notice:

- circular folds of the mucosa (known as plicae circulares)
- the green thread in the hepatopancreatic ampulla (where the common bile ductand pancreatic duct come together

The hepatopancreatic ampulla can also be seen in specimen **GI-5S3.** The common bile duct is visible as well.

Specimen **GI-5S6 (McM 904)** shows how the pancreas sits in relation to the duodenum. Notice how the head of the pancreas sits in the C-shaped curvature of the duodenum. Examine this specimen and identify the duodenum, pancreas, and common hepatic duct.

Specimen **GI5S1** also shows the pancreas. The pancreatic duct is more visible in this specimen however. The pancreas is composed of two types of tissue: 1) gland acini-produces pancreatic juice that is secreted into the duodenum; 2) Islets of Langerhans-solid buds that produce insulin and glucagons.

Exercise Two: Ileum/Jejunum

The small intestine is composed of the duodenum, jejunum and ileum. You saw the duodenum in station three, it re-enters the peritoneal cavity by the spleen and is considered by surgeons to end at the ligament of Trietz. The jejunum and ileum are entirely intra-peritoneal. The small intestine wall has multiple layers.

Look at specimen **GI6S7.** The serosa is the visceral peritoneum. The muscularis layer is the muscle layer composed of the inner circular fibers to narrow the lumen and the longitudinal muscle fibers to shorten the tube. *(note – this specimen shows a 3rd oblique layer of muscle which is only present in the stomach).* The submucosa is a layer of connective tissue where the blood vessels, nerves and glands are located. The mucosa is the innermost layer of the tract and is composed of superficial epithelium and glandular cells that secrete mucous and digestive juices.

The jejunum and ileum are slung by mesentery **(GI-6S1)** whose root is attached to the posterior abdominal wall. The jejunum is the upper 2/5 of the small intestine in the upper left of abdomen while the ileum is lower 3/5 of small intestine in the lower abdomen. Jejunum is characterized as well vascularized, with thick walls, mesenteric fat that does not go all the way over tube, and a lot of plicae circularis. The ileum has aggregated lymph follicles (Peyer's patches), decreasing plicae circularis such that the inside is flat by the end, and the mesenteric fat is abundant.

Examine specimen **GI6S6** and notice theses differences between the jejunum and ileum. The upper portion of the specimen is the jejunum and the lower potion is the ileum.

The blood supply to the small intestine comes from the superior mesenteric artery a branch of the abdominal aorta **(GI-6S3).**

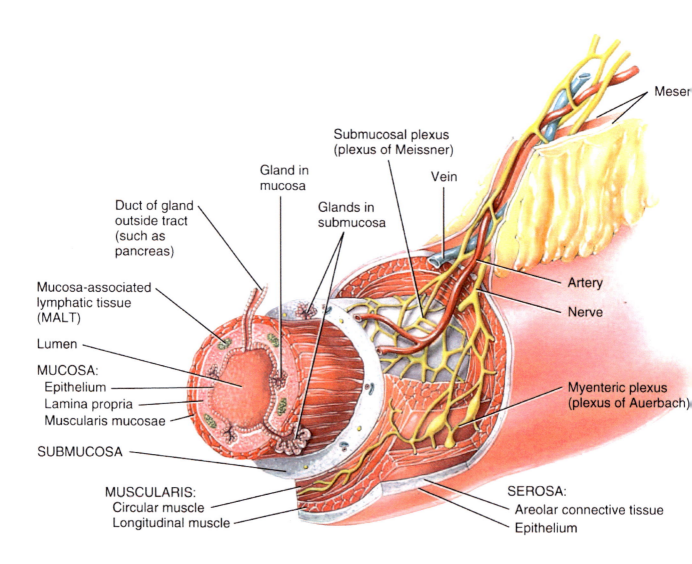

Figure 2 Layers of the small intestine.

Station Three: Liver and Gall Bladder

The liver is a large upper abdominal organ that lies below the diaphragm and under the cover of the ribs. The round ligament (ligamentum teres) is the degenerated umbilical vein. It runs in the falciform ligament to the liver. In the fetus, oxygenated blood bypasses the liver via the ductus venosus (which becomes the ligamentum venosum after birth) to run into the inferior vena cava. The hepatic portal system is how blood from the digestive organs (in superior mesenteric vein) and from blood cell destruction (in splenic vein) enters the portal vein and goes to the liver for detoxification before entering the inferior vena cava via the hepatic veins to return to the heart. This system ensures that all the nutrients absorbed by the intestines passes through the liver before entering the general circulation. It allows the liver to absorb and break down any toxins and to allow the immune cells in the liver to attack any invading microorganisms that entered the body through the intestinal tract.

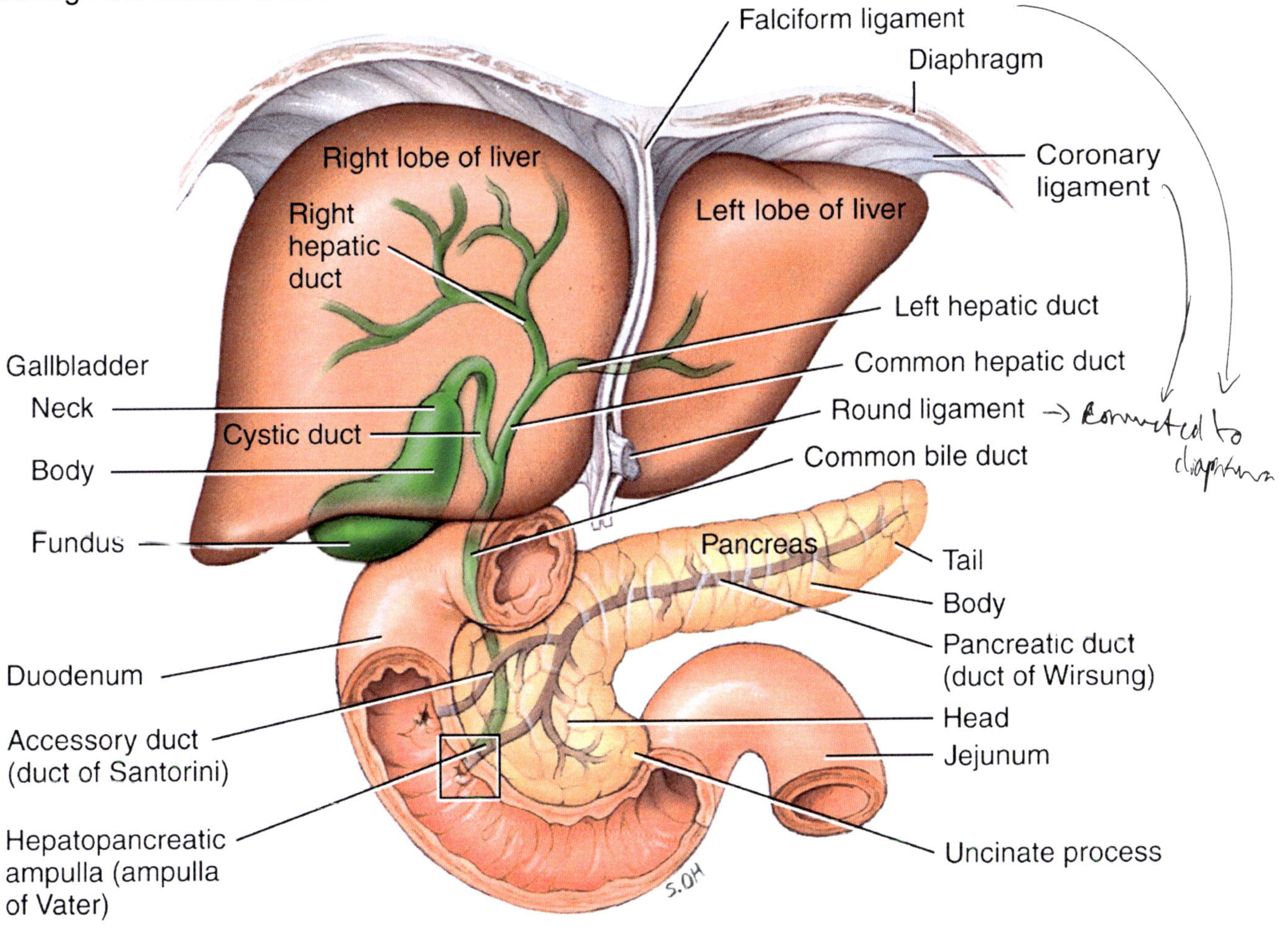

Figure 3. Liver, duodenum, and galbladder

The blood supply to the liver is through the left and right hepatic arteries.

Observe specimen **GI7S6 (McM 934 and McM 732)** to see the hepatic artery (red string), hepatic veins (blue strings entering the inferior vena cava), gall bladder (on the inferior of liver surface -open) and round ligament (between lobes).

Specimen **GI7S7** shows the gall bladder, which stores bile with the cystic duct opening into common hepatic duct. Blood supply to the Gall Bladder is through the cystic artery.

Identify the following on model and compare with specimen:
- Quadrate lobe (1)-Right bigger lobe
- Caudate lobe (2)-L smaller lobe
- Gall bladder (3)
- Round Ligament (Ligamentum teres) (4)-thick and round by falciform ligament
- Inferior Vena Cava (5)
- Falciform ligament (6)-separates two lobes and holds liver to anterior abdominal wall
- Cystic Duct (7) —gall bladder
- Left hepatic duct (point of junction with R hepatic duct and origin of common hepatic duct not visible) (8)
- Common Bile duct (9)
- Hepatic artery (10)
- Portal vein (11)
- Hepatic Vein (12)

An example of a pathology that can affect the gallbladder is gallstones. Specimen **GI8P(B)-S2 (McM 2130)** shows a gallbladder with multiple gallstones.

Cholesterol ↑   bilirubin ←

↑   ↓
White   red stones
stones

(Stones created
from excess solutes
(deposits))

hepatomegaly

bile canaliculi
↓
bile ductules
↓
bile duct
↓ ↓
common bile duct
↓
hepatic duct
↓
duodenum

Station Four: Large Intestine

The first section of the large intestine is called the caecum. The caecum is the balloon-like structure where the large intestine and small intestine meet. The junction between the ileum of the small intestine and cecum of the large intestine is the *ileocecal junction*. It has a ring of smooth muscle, the *ileocecal sphincter*, and a one way *ileocecal valve*. The ileocecal valve allows passage of chyme in a single direction. Also, the large intestine contains a great number of bacteria, therefore the ileo-caecal valve helps keep the ileum sterile.

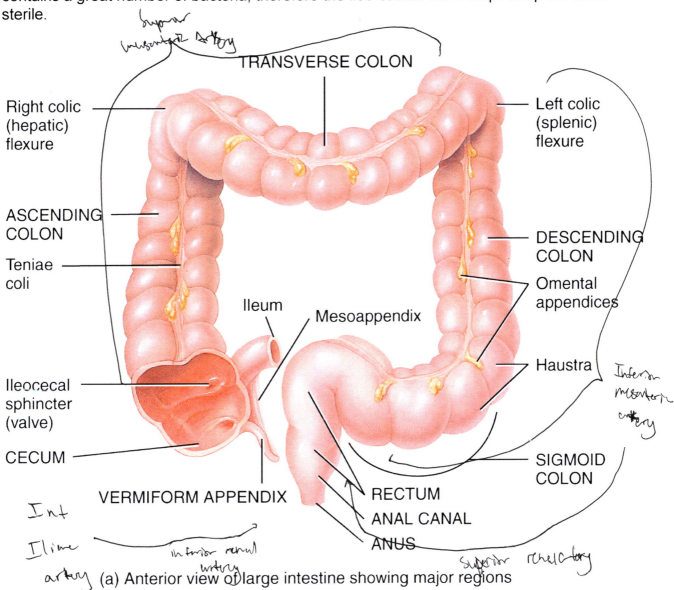

(a) Anterior view of large intestine showing major regions

Figure 4. Large intestine.

Projecting off the cecum is a blind out pocketing of the intestine called the **vermiform appendix**.

Observe this structure in specimen **GI10S1 (McM 2061)**. In herbivores, this acts as a repository for the bacteria that allow digestion of the cell walls of plants. In humans it is mostly vestigial, though it contains lymphoid tissue that allows it to combat inflammation. The 3 longitudinal bands of muscle running along the entire length of the colon all originate at the base of the appendix.

The cecum continues as the ascending colon. In the large intestine/colon the chyme is concentrated through the removal of water. The purpose of the colon is to prepare, store and pass fecal matter. Bacteria assist in the uptake of water, and also produce some vitamins that will be absorbed by the colon. Mucous produced in the distal colon assists in expulsion of the fecal matter.

The cecum, ascending colon, and descending colon, though covered with peritoneum on the anterior surface, lie directly on the posterior abdominal wall. The transverse colon and sigmoid colon are surrounded by peritoneum, which forms a mesentery termed the mesocolon for the transverse colon, and the sigmoid mesocolon for the sigmoid colon. The transverse mesocolon passes forward from the pancreas to enclose the transverse colon

Observe the radiograph **GI10-C4** to see the colon/large intestine which runs along the margins of the abdominal cavity, originating at the lower right hand quadrant. The caecum extends into the ascending colon, which changes direction at the right or hepatic flexure to extend across the abdomen as the transverse colon. The colon then bends sharply downward (the left or splenic flexure) to become the descending colon, the sigmoid colon then, as it enters the true pelvis, the rectum and anal canal.

Three bands of thickened smooth muscle run the length of the colon called the **teniae coli.**

Observe specimen **GI10S2 (McM 943 and McM 2231)**. They appear ribbonlike, and draw the large intestine into pouchlike folds called haustra. Fat is arranged on the surface of the large intestine in epiploic appendages.

There are three main functions of the large intestine, to consolidate waste matter, the site of production of vitamins B and K, and reabsorption of water and electrolytes. There are three sphincters, the ileocal valve, and the internal and external anal sphincters. The superior and inferior mesenteric arteries supply the majority of the large intestine. These originate from the aorta. The inferior mesenteric artery supplies the left of the transverse colon distally, and gives a branch, which forms the superior rectal. The inferior rectal artery is a branch of the internal iliac artery.

Vulvulus → single pouch created by the pivot off of the large intestine. No blood flow to it.

diverticulosis → multiple pouches created by different pressure at the intestine,

Case Study/Pathology

William is a 65 year old CEO who has always enjoyed his steaks and red wine. He has thrown himself into his work his entire life and never made time to exercise or make healthy meals. William has been experiencing bloating and abdominal pain recently. His Dr. orders a CT scan and thinks she has found the source of his trouble.

Examine specimen **GI-10P-S5**

What portion of the GI system is this?

Large Intestine

Compare this specimen to a "healthy" one. What differences do you see?

several outpouches growt on the intestine

Based on this comparison, what disease process do you think is occurring?

diverticulitis

Lab 5

Renal Systems and Reproductive Systems

Objectives for Station 1 and 2:
The objective of this lab is to gain an understanding of renal anatomy and physiology and to perform experiments to test the contents of normal and "pathological" urine. Students should gain an understanding of the positioning of the kidney in the body, the arrangement of renal arteries and veins, the ureter in both the male and female, and the bladder/urethra positioning in both the male and the female.

Station One: Anatomy of the Kidney

Keyword List:

KIDNEY: Renal Hilus, Cortex
MEDULLA: Renal Pyramids, Minor Calyces, Major Calyces, Renal Pelvis
BLADDER: Trigone, Ureter
ARTERIES: Renal

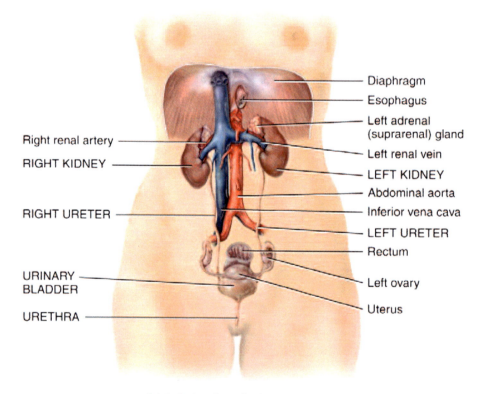

(a) Anterior view of urinary system

Figure 1 The urinary system

The kidneys are retroperitoneal organs, which lie on the back body wall between thoracic vertebrae 12 (T12) and lumbar vertebrae 2 (L2). The right one is slightly lower than the left one due to the liver pushing it down.

Observe their location on the torso model and specimen. The kidneys are supplied by the renal artery, which is a branch of the abdominal aorta and are drained by renal veins.

Observe **UG0 819** and **UG1S9**. The arteries and veins enter and leave the kidney via the renal hilus. The renal artery sends 5 segmental arteries into the kidney. The ureter, lymph vessels and nerve fibers also pass through the renal hilus. One specimen shows the kidney with the renal artery entering it. The other specimen is a resin cast of the blood supply of the kidney, demonstrating its extensiveness.

The kidney is surrounded by perinephric fat (**UG1-S2**). This fat is important in protecting the kidney and allowing the kidneys to move around during changes in body posture and respiration. The fat surrounds the posterior and sides of the kidney.

What are the two main divisions of the kidney and how can you differentiate between them? The two main divisions of the kidney are the cortex and the medulla (**UG0 830**). The cortex is the more outer section of the kidney and is lighter brown while the medulla is the more inner section of the kidney and is a darker brown. The medulla is made up of renal pyramids. These pyramids have their base near the cortex. Minor calyces cup the apex of the pyramids. The cortex projects between the pyramids, these projections are called renal columns. Compare the specimen and model present. Notice the difference between the cortex and medulla is visible in the specimen.

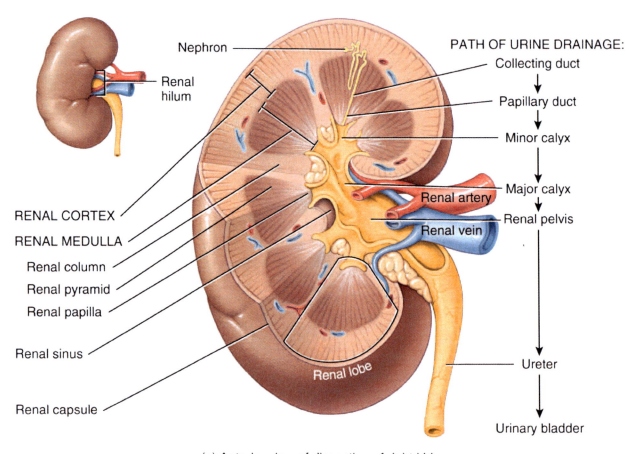

Nephron

Renal hilum

PATH OF URINE DRAINAGE:
Collecting duct
Papillary duct
Minor calyx
Major calyx
Renal artery
Renal pelvis
Renal vein
Ureter
Urinary bladder

RENAL CORTEX
RENAL MEDULLA
Renal column
Renal pyramid
Renal papilla
Renal sinus
Renal lobe
Renal capsule

(a) Anterior view of dissection of right kidney

Figure 2. Internal Anatomy of the Kidney

Urine is transported to the bladder via the ureter. The ureters are muscular tubes that leave the kidneys via the renal hilum and enter the bladder on its posterior surface at an angle. They move urine via peristaltic contractions. They are about 10 inches in length (about the same length as the esophagus. The ureters enter the bladder at an angle forming a valve like structure preventing the back flow of urine.

Observe specimen **UG4PS6**.

Kidney Stones

What do you think this condition is called and what are the problems associated with this condition? This condition is called nephrolithiasis or more commonly kidney stones. Most stones form from calcium oxalate and phosphate, but they can be from uric acid or proteins as well. Kidney stones vary in size from very small ones, which can be passed (although painfully) to larger ones (such as the ones seen here). Kidney stones may obstruct urine outflow, which can lead to infection. Smaller stones may get stuck where the ureter enters the bladder. Larger stones may block the renal pelvis. In this specimen the pelvis is almost filled by stones.

Station Two: Urinalysis

Objective: You should understand the function of the nephron and collecting ducts and how the analysis of urine is useful in the evaluation of health and disease.

SAFETY ALERT
FACULTY OF HEALTH SCIENCES McMASTER UNIVERSITY

Universal Precautions Applying to Blood, Bodily Fluids and Tissues
1.   Gloves, lab coats and protective eyewear must be worn when coming in contact with blood or bodily fluids.
2.   Wash hands when contaminated or immediately after gloves are removed.
3.   Take precautions to avoid injuries with sharp instruments.
4.   Use only mechanical pipetting devices.
5.   Decontaminate work surfaces daily and after spills. Use 1 in 10 household bleach, 70% ethanol, or alternative germicide
6.   Remove all lab coats or other protective equipment before leaving the lab.

Materials:
1urine sample cup

Methods

1.   Take the urine sample cup to the washroom and collect a 100- 200 ml urine sample. To get a "clean catch" it is necessary to void a small amount of urine and then collect the next 100-200 ml. There are no prizes for the fullest specimen cup.

   - Take a urine specimen bottle to the washroom.
   - Wash and dry hands thoroughly.
   - Remove lid from container and set lid upside down.
   - **DO NOT TOUCH THE INNER SURFACE.**
   - Pass a small amount of urine into the toilet, then void into container.
   - **DO NOT TOUCH CONTAINER OPENING.**
   - Secure lid tightly
   - Wash and dry hands thoroughly.
   - Return container to laboratory.

Exercise One: Physical Examination

1.   *Quantity.*

This test is normally carried out over a time to determine the rate of urine production. There are many factors which can increase urine production including, diabetes, chronic infections, excessive fluid intake and diuretics. More worrisome than high urine production is low urine production. The factors that can lead to an abnormally low rate of urine production are acute infections, low fluid intake, dehydration, and shock.

2.   *Colour.*

Normal urine is a pale yellow fluid. Abnormal urine is often red or brown. Red indicates blood (hematuria) or hemoglobin (hemoglobinuria).

3.   *Transparency*

Normal urine is clear. The presence of cloudiness or "smoke" indicates suspended material such as mucus, bacteria or various types of cells.

> Once you have collected a urine sample in Exercise One, you can record the physical properties in Chart 1.

Chart 1: Physical Properties

colour _____

clarity _____

Exercise Two: Chemical Examination

In this section you will be using Multistix, a commercially prepared reagent strip that tests a urine sample for all of the factors listed below. Most of these tests are useful for screening purposes and are not very accurate or precise. They are, however, easily and quickly carried out so they may give many hints about underlying pathology.

pH: Urine pH ranges from 5-9 and is often around 6, or slightly acidic. Persistent low urinary pH usually indicates renal compensation for high H+ concentration of the blood.

protein: Protein concentration in the urine is normally beneath the detection limit of the Multistix. The presence of protein is called **proteinuria** and this can be caused by a number of kidney pathologies as well urinary tract infection.

glucose: There is not normally any glucose in the urine, however, when the reabsorption capacity of the kidney for glucose is exceeded glucose may remain in the kidney tubules and enter the urine. This condition is called **glycosuria** and is associated with diabetes mellitus (insulin-dependent diabetes), liver disease or certain endocrine disorders. In pregnancy a certain amount of glycosuria is common so pregnancy is often called a diabetogenic state.

ketones: The test area for ketones reacts with acetoacetic acid and acetone. These byproducts of lipid metabolism are always found in the blood in low concentration but not normally in the urine. Insulin dependent diabetics and others who suffer from abnormal carbohydrate metabolism often exhibit **ketonuria**, the presence of "ketone bodies", actually acetone, acetoacetic acid and hydroxybutyric acid, in the urine.

urobilinogen: This is a byproduct of hemoglobin degradation. Bilirubin is normally absorbed from the blood as it passes through the liver and is then excreted in the bile. The bile is released into the small intestine. In the large intestine the bilirubin may be converted into urobilinogen which can be reabsorbed back into to the blood. Small amounts of urobilinogen in the urine are, therefore, normal. In fact the characteristic yellow colour of urine is due to a heme breakdown product called urochrome. High levels of urobilinogen indicate large quantities of heme are being broken down.

blood: The tests on the Multistix detect urine hemoglobin (*hemoglobinuria*) and red blood cells (*hematuria*). The presence of blood in the urine is abnormal and may be the result of kidney or urinary tract disease. Blood is often detected in the urine of menstruating women but it is a result of sloppy sample collection, not urinary blood.

WBCs: The presence of a large number of white blood cells in the urine is a clear indicator of urinary tract infection or, more seriously, kidney infection. The reagent test on the Multistix is quite inadequate to detect urinary tract infections in about 80 % of women.

Nitrite: The conversion of nitrate, which is a common component of urine, to nitrite by gram-negative bacteria (like *E. coli*, the commonest cause of urinary tract infection). If urine has not remained in the bladder for sufficient time for nitrite production, the test will always be negative. This is one of the urine tests that should be done with the first voided sample in the morning.

Specific gravity (actually considered a physical property): the weight of urine compared to an equal amount of water. The normal range of specific gravity for human urine is 1.015 to 1.020 so urine is normally denser than water. High solute load in the urine can increase its density.

Materials:
1 Multistix * SG urinalysis reagent strip

Methods

You will be carrying out the chemical analysis on the urine sample obtained for Exercise One.

1.   The Multistix are kept in an airtight jar. Remove one strip from the bottle and replace the cap.   Always handle the strips by the plastic handle and not by the reagent area
2.   Immerse the reagent strip in the urine sample and remove. Tap the side of the specimen cup with the reagent strip to remove any drops of urine.
3.   Hold the strip horizontally and then compare each test area at the appropriate time. Record results in the following chart.
4.   After 10 minutes reread the urinalysis strip. Note which results have changed.

Once you have examined the urine sample in Exercise Two, you can record the chemical properties in Chart 2.

Chart 2 – Urinalysis: Chemical Properties

Test	Reading Time	Result
Glucose	30 s	
Ketones	40 s	
Specific Gravity	45s	
Blood	1 min	
pH	1 min	
Protein	1 min	
Nitrite	1 min	
Leucocytes	2 min	

1. Wash the remaining urine down the sink with plenty of water (Unless you wish   do complete the microscope examination).
2. Wash the bench area with 10% bleach solution.
3. Dispose of sample containers, gloves, and Multistix in biohazard box.

*********FYI: Microscopic Examination************

This exercise IS NOT a part of Station 2. For those interested, this component of the lab can be completed when all of the other stations are complete. Please ask Christiane for assistance BEFORE YOU BEGIN this exercise.

Examination of the particulate components of urine, i.e., the sediment, is a common means of diagnosis. Though it is difficult to identify all that makes up the sediment you should be able to see crystals of various descriptions and epithelial cells which have been shed from the kidneys and urinary tract. The presence of RBCs leucocytes and bacteria are all clinically significant findings and have been discussed in Part B. You may be able to see **casts** which are agglomerations of blood cells or protein in the shape of a kidney tubule. The number and shape of casts can be useful in diagnosing a number of pathologies.

Materials:
1 conical bottomed centrifuge tube, 1 microscope, 1 slide, 1 cover slip

Methods:

1. Fill a conical centrifuge tube with urine to within 2 cm of the top. Balance the centrifuge volume by eye with another group. Put the two tubes in opposite buckets (i.e., 180° apart). The teaching assistants will operate the centrifuge.

2. Pour off the supernatant and add a drop of "Sedistain" to the solid material in the bottom of the tube.

3. Mix the stain and sediment by horizontally striking the outside of the centrifuge tube.

4. Pour one drop of the mixture on a slide and cover with a coverslip.

5. Examine the mixture with the low power lens and then with high power under oil immersion.

6. Record your results in the following chart 3.

CHART 3: Urinalysis Microscope Examination

Material in Urine Sediment	Picture	Relative Abundance
Epithelial Cells		
Leukocytes		
RBC's		
Crystals		

Bacteria		
Casts		
Other		

Station Three: Female Reproductive System

Objective:
To become familiar with the structures involved with the female reproductive system. The lab will also focus on understanding the functional anatomy of the reproductive tract and the physiology of reproduction.

Keyword List:

Female:

Uterus:
Fallopian or Uterine tubes
Round Ligament
Broad Ligament

Ovaries:
Ovarian Ligament
Suspensory Ligament

Cervix
Vagina

External Genitalia:
Clitoris
Labia Minora
Labia Majora

Arteries:
UterineArtery
Ovarian Artery

Exercise One: Female Reproductive Anatomy

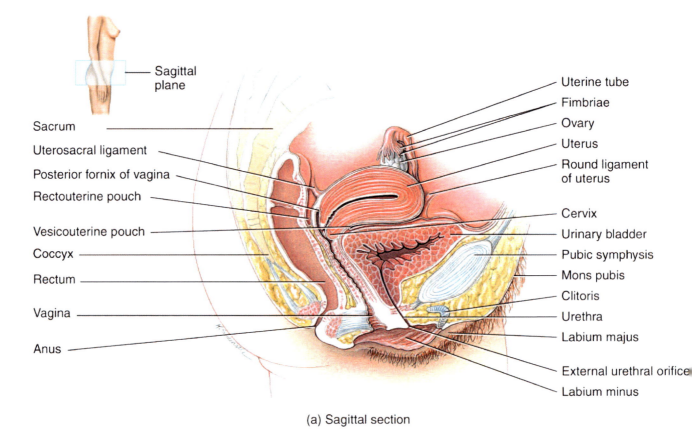

(a) Sagittal section

Figure 3. Female reproductive anatomy.

Observe the **block** containing the uterus and ovaries. Note that the paired ovaries flank the uterus on each side.

What is the function of the ovaries?

Identify the duct system associated with the ovaries and name the 4 regions of this duct system.
Can you name the blood supply that serves the ovaries and identify how it reaches

the ovaries.

Observe model **PE3S6**. Note the position and location of the uterus. The uterus lies anterior to the rectum and posterosuperior to the bladder. The uterus is antiverted where it joins the vagina and antiflexed where it joins the cervix.

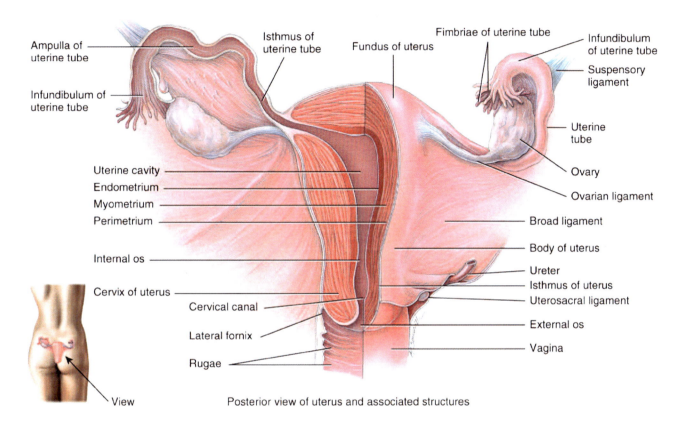

Figure 4. Internal Organs of reproduction in the female.

The ovaries and uterus are supported and held in place by a number of ligaments. Identify the following ligaments in specimen **PE2S3** and where they attach to:

1.   ovarian ligament – anchors the ovary medially to the superior margin of the uterus.

2.   suspensory ligament – anchors the ovary laterally to the pelvic wall.

3.   round ligament – anchors the uterus anteriorly to the anterior body wall.
4.   uterosacral ligament (not shown in our textbook) – anchors the uterus posteriorly to the sacrum.
5.   broad ligament – peritoneal fold extending from the lateral margin of the uterus to the wall of the pelvis on either side

Case Study/Pathology

Maddy is a 23 year old who has been sexually active for about 3 years. She has always been forgetful when it came to taking her oral contraceptive pills so was looking into other methods of contraception.

Examine specimen PE-5-S9 and identify the uterus, cervix, and fallopian tubes

What is the device inserted into the uterus and how do you think it might work as a contraceptive device?

Copper iud → copper → toxic to sperm
→ brings in white blood cells.

hormonal iud → releases progestogen, prevents ovulation.
→ produces cervical membrane (mucus)

Exercise Two: Female pelvis

Examine the **model of the female pelvis**. The true pelvis is located inferior to the pelvic brim. The false pelvis extends above the pelvic brim, between the two iliac wings.

What is the shape of the female pelvis? How is this different from the male pelvis?

oval   arc shaped

Which boney structures loosen to allow greater flexibility of the pelvis and greater size of the true pelvis during pregnancy? Do you know why they loosen?

pubic symphysis

iliosacral

sacryl coccynal

Station Four: Male Reproductive Anatomy

Objective:
To become familiar with the structures involved with the male reproductive system. The lab will also focus on understanding the functional anatomy of the reproductive tract and the physiology of reproduction.

Keyword List: Male:
Inguinal canal

Arteries:
Testicular artery (gonadal artery)

Penis:
Crus of Penis
Corpus spongiosum
Corpus cavernosum

Testis:
Tunica Vaginalis
Scrotum
Tunica Albuginea
Epididymis
Tubulus rectus
Ductus deferens
Seminiferous tubules
Rete Testes
Efferent ductules
Cremaster muscle

Glands:
Seminal vesicles
Prostate
Bulbourethral glands
Ejaculatory duct

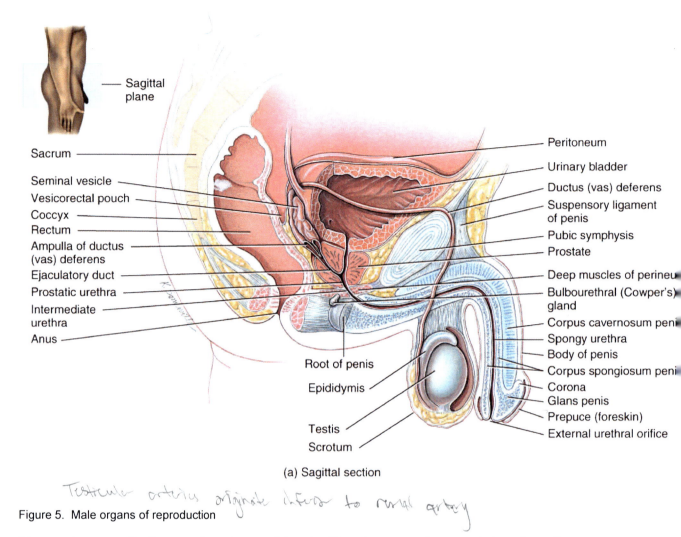

Sagittal plane

Sacrum

Seminal vesicle
Vesicorectal pouch
Coccyx
Rectum
Ampulla of ductus (vas) deferens
Ejaculatory duct
Prostatic urethra
Intermediate urethra
Anus

Root of penis
Epididymis
Testis
Scrotum

Peritoneum
Urinary bladder
Ductus (vas) deferens
Suspensory ligament of penis
Pubic symphysis
Prostate
Deep muscles of perineu
Bulbourethral (Cowper's) gland
Corpus cavernosum peni
Spongy urethra
Body of penis
Corpus spongiosum peni
Corona
Glans penis
Prepuce (foreskin)
External urethral orifice

(a) Sagittal section

Testicular artery originate inferior to renal artery

Figure 5. Male organs of reproduction

The male reproductive system is combined with urinary system and develops from Wolfian duct system in the embryo. The gonads develop in an area which becomes the kidney in the developing fetus. The gonad travels inferiorly and exits the abdominal cavity through the internal inguinal ring, the inguinal canal and then the external inguinal ring to take its permanent place in the scrotum usually in the last few weeks before birth. The traction on the gonads necessary to pull them out of the abdomen is applied by the gubernaculums which are paired fibrous cords located on the inferior surface of the testicle.

Why are undescended testicles more common in premature babies?
Doesn't descent till last stages of germination

What are the implications if the testicle fails to descend? (ie chryptorchidism.)
Chryptochidism is the most common congenital deformity. The undescended testicle will fail to be able to produce <u>viable sperm</u>, since the critical temperature for sperm development is slightly below body temperature. Partially descended testicles may be lying in front of the pubic bone, making the testicle itself prone to traumatic injury.

Observe specimen **GI11S5** which shows the inguinal region. Note the spermatic cord comes through the external inguinal ring on each side.

What is also located in the inguinal ring on the patient's right side? This is peritoneum, potentially covering a loop of intestine. This might be an inguinal hernia in the making. A hernia is when a loop of intestine is forced from its normal location in the abdominal cavity. Other "weak spots" in the abdominal wall where this can occur include the umbilical region, and the hiatus of the diaphragm

Observe specimen **UG1S10**.

inferior to renal artery

Where does the arterial supply for the testicle originate? Why is the testicular artery so high in the abdomen?

Exercise One: Testes

The testes are surrounded by the scrotum, the tunica vaginalis (an extension of the lining of the abdominal cavity, the peritoneum), and, most intimately the tunica albuginea. The latter is a white fibrous coat, which is not elastic. Expansion of a testis due to swelling is particularly painful because the tunica albuginea does not expand thus pressure is kept high in the scrotum which is a painful stimulus.

PE3S16 demonstrates the external genitalia and the layers of the testicle. Can you identify: **the skin, superficial fat and fascia, the dartos muscle** (small muscle fibres located within the superficial fascia which constrict the scrotum in the cold), **the cremaster muscle** (sheet of muscle that contracts when the testicles are cold thus raising them towards the main body to warm up), **and the tunica vaginalis** (a double fold of peritoneum that traveled surrounding the testicle in its journey from its original placement in the abdominal cavity below the kidney?

Superior to the testicle is the epididymis. This is a comma-shaped tubule where immotile sperm gain motility and are stored. It is a coiled tubule with an uncoiled length of approximately 6 meters. Its head is located on the superior aspect of the testicle, and its tail extends down the posteriolateral aspect of the testicle. The ductus deferens is the continuation of its tail. The testicle itself is formed of seminiferous tubules arranged into 250-300 lobulues. The tubules converge to form common tubules termed the tubulus rectus, which in turn form the rete testis. The rete testis leaves the testicle through the efferent ductules, and enters the epididymis. On the **specimen of the testicle**, identify the testicular artery, the ductus deferens, the seminiferous tubules and the epididymus

Exercise Two: Male Urethra (PE3S11) And Accessory Glands

The male urethra begins as the prostatic urethra within the prostate **(PE1S7),** a walnut sized structure described in more detail below. The seminal vesicles, and the ductus deferens (also known as the vas deferens or simply the vas) form the ejaculatory duct, which comes together with the urethra within the prostate. Once the urethra leaves the prostate, it travels about 1.5 cm as the membranous urethra. This region is particularly delicate, and is on an angle with respect to the penile urethra. Caution must be taken during catheterization not to damage the membranous urethra. It is surrounded by sphincter muscles, and is the least dilatable part of the urethra. The urethra then enters the bulb and then corpus spongeosum of the penis. It is called the penile urethra at this point and measures approx. 15 cm. The penile urethra continues to the external meatus which is the narrowest part of the male urethra. The urethra ends at the fossa terminalis inside of the glans penis. This segment is dilated and lined with epidermis.

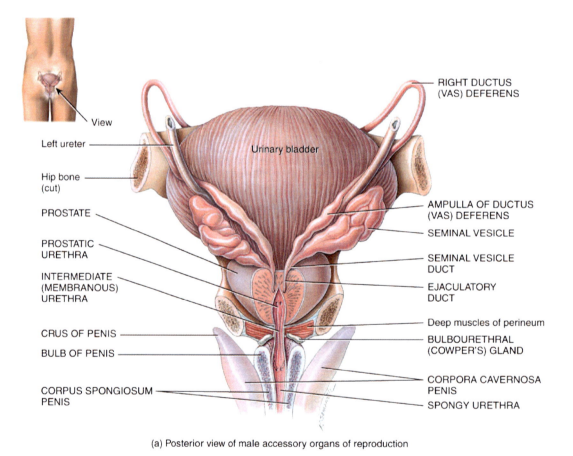

(a) Posterior view of male accessory organs of reproduction

Figure 6. Accessory organs reproduction in the male.

The prostate gland consists of five lobes, which are different not only with respect to their location, but with respect to their susceptibility to prostatic hyperplasia and tumors. It is located just anterior to the rectum, allowing for examination, and possible operation for prostatic disease. The prostate is isolated by muscles from the urinary bladder during intercourse. The bulbourethral glands (Cowper's Glands) are located just posterior to the membranous urethra.

As mentioned, the vas deferens terminates at the prostate gland and meets the seminal vesicles at the ejaculatory duct. While the vas transports the sperm, it is semen which is necessary for a normal ejaculate. Semen is a mixture of a number of different materials which protect and nurture the sperm. The seminal vesicles provide about 60% of semen volume. The seminal vesicles provide an alkaline media which will neutralize the normally acidic male urethra and female vaginal lumen. Further, the seminal vesicles provide nutrients for the sperm in the form of fructose as well as clotting proteins so the semen can clot within the vagina and not leak back out. Ultimately the clot must break down so that the sperm can escape. The prostate provides the clot-busting proteins as well as some nutrient for the sperm. The prostate also produces prostaglandins (hence the name). These appear to have some effect on uterine contractions which may aid in propelling sperm towards the uterine tubes. The final contributor to the ejaculate are the bulbourethral glands which are pea-sized gland found to the sides of the prostate. These glands produce an alkaline mucus which neutralizes the acidity of the urethra and provides some modest amounts of lubrication which allow for smoother passage of the sperm out of the urethra.

Exercise Three: Penis

The penis itself is primarily formed by three cylindrical bodies of erectile tissue, surrounded by tunica albuginea.

Observe specimen **PE3S17**. The dorsal two provide turgidity during erection and are termed the corpus caveronsa. Their proximal ends are surrounded by the ischiocavernosus muscle and are thereby anchored to the pubic arch of the bony pelvis. They form the crus peni. The third cylindrical body, called the corpus spongiosum surrounds the urethra and forms the glans penis. To prevent constriction of the urethra, it does not get as engorged with blood as the corpus cavernosa.

What is the blood supply to the penis?

What is the path of the sperm from seminiferous tubule to external environment?